*This book is dedicated to all the pupils and staff at
Five Acre Wood School, Maidstone.*

Definition

TNT - A Tiny Noticeable Thing that nobody needs to do, but when somebody does do it, it creates an explosive, highly impactful image that exceeds expectations and makes a very big difference. The shock-waves generated by such an act are both profound and long lasting. Thinking is reshaped and relationships transformed.

> *"The smallest act of kindness is worth more than the grandest intention."*
> —Oscar Wilde

Contents

Acknowledgments

An enormous thank you to all those of you who have been kind enough to share your TNTs.

With special thanks to my niece Lisa Gledhill for her encouragement for me to write this book and to Richard Hannah for helping me get started.

Thanks also to Karen Turton, Lindsey Rowe, Jaime Jukes, Stuart Holah, Tim Williams, Andrea Charlton, Mal Watkins and Peter Walklate for cheering me on!

And, to my good friend James Poole for his enduring patience and unwavering support along the way.

Finally, hats off to my daughter Rosie for all her creative input.

In memory of Barry Webster and Honey The Beagle-"Beagsley"

Introduction

Tiny Noticeable Things

TNTs are *Tiny Noticeable Things*. They are all the little things that people don't need to do, but *do* do.

They may be tiny, but they are highly explosive, and they create the biggest, longest-lasting and most vivid of pictures in people's minds.

They are the difference between a four- and five-star customer experience; the difference between a manager and a leader; the difference between a team that's floundering and a team that's flying. They are the difference between a great place to work and a not-so-great place. They show how much we care; they make and break relationships, and yet they cost nothing.

They could be as small as a smile, as teeny as a 'thank you', perhaps remembering a person's first name or recalling if a customer prefers their coffee with or without sugar. Maybe a few words of encouragement or even a handwritten note of recognition to a team member. Tiny, simple things that are overlooked all too often but have the potential to set in motion seismic shifts in thinking and bring about profound change. The effect that these little engagers can have is quite phenomenal.

Their explosive power comes from the fact that they are out-of-the-blue, unexpected, surprising acts of kindness. They are those little extra steps that people take for each other that go beyond expectations. Their impact is so much so that they are able to penetrate straight through the conscious mind and gain fast-track access to the subconscious, where they detonate – triggering deep, dormant emotions.

Used effectively, they light up faces, electrify rooms and make people's days. Whether you are looking to energise and inspire your teams, put customers at the heart of everything you do, get ahead of the competition or just blow someone away – never underestimate the potent power of TNTs.

TNTs – The Difference

Before going full-time on the speaking circuit, I spent most of my career in a commercial environment trying to get the very best out of people. I was forever looking for innovative ways to engage and motivate teams of everyday people like myself to pull together and deliver extraordinary results.

As a team, we were constantly searching for opportunities to make a real difference for our customers with the services we had to offer. They were always challenging times with massive targets to meet, huge amounts of competition and recruitment firms trying to steal our best people.

Not having the deep pockets that our bigger competitors appeared to have, or for that matter any particularly unique product to sell, we somehow had to stand out in what was a ferociously competitive marketplace. To make this happen, in addition to doing all the basics consistently well, we had to continually step beyond our customers' expectations by doing all the little extra, standout things – the 'tiny noticeable things' – far better than any of our competitors. Hence, out of necessity to deliver and exceed expectations, 'TNTs' were born, and as a team fanatical about creating exceptional customer experiences – they soon became our secret weapon to making a difference.

For me, whether we're talking about inspirational leadership, building high-performance winning teams or delivering outstanding customer service, it's all about how we make people feel – great people make people feel great, and when it comes to making people feel great, nothing is as effective as TNTs.

These days, whether I'm delivering keynote presentations or running workshops, no matter what topics are covered or the size of organisation I am speaking to, TNTs are always the biggest and most popular takeaway with delegates. Probably because they are so easy to implement, they make an instant difference, and, being such simple things, everybody gets behind them. A regular feedback comment being: 'I now have a name for all those little things that I've always been aware of but just didn't know what they were called before!' When listening to people in group discussions talking about their own past personal experiences, I am reminded of just how important TNT moments can be. It's fascinating to hear about how the smallest gestures, that at the time seemed relatively unimportant and of no real significance, now mean so much. It's never the big stuff that is reminisced about; it's always the briefest interactions that touch hearts, stick in minds, influence thinking and leave the greatest impressions.

TNTs Shared

During some of the sessions I run, both the most 'popular' positive and negative TNTs that are encountered on a daily basis are discussed. As you can probably imagine, the number of negative ones, those that irritate and wind people up, always outweigh the ones that delight. The consensus of opinion being that, with all of us living in an increasingly fast-paced, automated world, and with everyone around us appearing to be in such a hurry all the time, human interaction is rapidly on the decline. Evidently, TNTs that make us smile are becoming scarcer.

In a quest to create more awareness of TNTs, encourage greater appreciation of their true value, and try and halt, if not reverse, their decline, I decided to shine some light on them by asking people to share their TNT moments in their own words. The following pages are a collection of some of those that I have received so far. They are either TNTs that people have experienced themselves or ones that they have done for others. As you will see, they come in many shapes and sizes, forms and guises, but what they all have in common is that, no matter how small they may appear or how insignificant they may sound, for somebody somewhere, they made a big difference.

All contributors have kindly given me permission to share their first-hand, personal stories with you. They are divided broadly into four categories: *Customer*, *Team*, *Personal* and *Covid*. In between these real-life experiences, I will be sharing my own thoughts as well as offering a few ideas as to how I think we can best motivate people to want to fully embrace TNTs and put them to good use.

Hopefully, this book will encourage you to share my passion for TNTs as well as inspire you to think even more about what small differences you can make each day, both in and out of the workplace. Quite possibly, random acts of kindness that give a little lift now and then to those most in need of one will become less random.

People will forget what you said, people will forget what you did, but people will never forget how you made them feel.
                                                                Maya Angelou

1

Customer

A customer's interpretation of any experience they have had will be based largely on whatever TNTs they at the time observed and how those TNTs added up and made them feel. We humans may struggle to take on board big things but what we are really good at doing is observing lots of little things, cumulative things that build impressions or corroborate our preconceived expectations.

Like most people, I live a fairly hectic life. Weekdays in particular are spent running around, juggling work and family, giving everything my best shot, most of the time remaining below radar, pretty much unnoticed. The level of customer service I receive tends to fluctuate between nondescript and okay, with the disappointing experiences sadly being, for the most part, the most memorable. The occasional, really good TNT experiences that I do have are few and far between and are the much-cherished exceptions that I can count on one hand over the space of a year. The reality being that, for the majority of the time, I am made to feel invisible, frequently getting the distinct sense that I am merely being robotically 'dealt with' or 'processed', rather than being 'served'. But, being so busy and just wanting to move on, I tolerate it, and having been exposed to so much of it for so long, I've got used to it, I've become immune. Mediocre service has become the norm, it is what I expect.

For those of us trying to differentiate ourselves by putting customers at the heart of everything we do and deliver stand-out service for all the right reasons, this really is fantastic news! If everyone was getting the TNTs right and blowing our socks off all the time, it would make standing out extremely difficult. However, with non-engaging, faceless service being so ubiquitous and people's expectations so low, there is now, more than ever before, an enormous opportunity that is ripe for the taking. When we do show how much we care by making time to do all the little things that we don't need to do, the more impactful they are, the more bowled over people are, and the more they go away and tell others about us. All sparked off by a few simple, zero-cost TNT actions. With so many organisations out there sleepwalking, doing things the way they've always done them, seemingly content with merely 'meeting' uninspired expectations, it's no wonder great TNTs have become so scarce. What so many businesses just don't appear to understand is that the tiniest of positive human interactions is all it takes to initiate some wonderful, lasting relationships and for them to be regarded as being outstanding because people love interacting with them.

The best news of all though about being outstanding is that you don't have to stand out way beyond any of your competition; you only have to stand out by the smallest of fractions. With most market sectors being so ultra-competitive, the reality is you'll probably never ever be streets ahead of your closest competitor – you don't need to be. So long as you are just one shoe size step ahead, you're ahead – and you will stand out!

What separates the few and far between organisations who have gained world-class reputations for creating an exceptional experience is that they know it's all about one thing – it's about going beyond their customers' expectations. With this at the forefront of their minds, all their people are motivated to continuously and proactively look for TNT opportunities to surprise and delight customers. They understand that, by always viewing themselves through the eyes of their customers, they are able to anticipate and then exceed expectations and that, each time they do that, that's when the magic happens. That's when a TNT detonates. A BOOM! is heard, and another customer goes away with their face beaming in delight. It not only makes the customer feel great, it makes them, the service provider, feel good too. Their days become so much more enjoyable, the weeks fly by and what they do for a living no longer feels like a job. And here's the key – this will only ever happen if all your people fully grasp this. They have to really want to make customers feel special, and the sooner they realise that by doing so, they too will feel several inches taller, the quicker it will happen.

The expression 'we treat our customers like old friends that we've not seen for a while' is one I hear over and over again from those who are passionate about customer care. When looking after customers, what is critical is that everybody in the team be not only committed but also accountable for doing it. Absolutely everyone needs to play their part and take ownership for doing their bit. No matter what their job title or level of seniority, everyone in the team needs to be permanently primed and ready to anticipate any potential needs a customer may have – every customer touchpoint moment needs to be seen as an opportunity to shine and stand out. No matter how hard an entire army of people may work behind the scenes, no matter how good the reputation that precedes them is or how deeply they may actually care, it only takes one TNT encounter with one slightly disengaged individual staff member to start painting a very big, memorable negative image. Every single person, whether they are customer facing or non-customer facing needs to be onboard and fully tuned into exploring ways to gently apply extra, subtle touches – thereby surpassing customer's expectations. In fact, I would go even further and say that it is probably more important that people perceived as being 'backroom staff' need to be more aware of TNTs and the effect they can have. There are two reasons for this. First, when a customer does get an occasional peek behind the scenes, the things they get to glimpse tend to carry far more weight in their minds because they feel they are witnessing a true, honest and transparent picture of what that business or organisation is really all about. Second, when they encounter a staff member that they regard as not being customer facing, their expectation of how engaging they are going to be is more likely to be different to that of what in their mind is a jolly, all-smiles customer-facing person. So, when they do interact with someone in a support role and that person is incredibly helpful and friendly, that experience is likely to be more genuine, sincere and powerful. 'Backroom' TNTs are without doubt the most highly explosive of all, yet despite creating such indelible impressions, they are invariably overlooked, the reality being that the most effort for improving customer experience generally tends to be focused 'front of house'.

As an example of TNTs being used at their absolute best, I'd like to share with you the experience I had whilst staying away for the first time ever at The Gleneagles Hotel in Scotland. I had just started out on the speaker circuit and had gone there to deliver a presentation.

Having checked in in the morning and spoken in the afternoon, I was walking past the reception in the evening when one of the receptionists smiled at me and said, 'Good evening, Mr Webster. How are you?' I am not only pleasantly surprised that they have remembered my name, but also wondering if perhaps I am still wearing my name badge from the conference. A quick glance down confirmed that I wasn't! Then the receptionist asked, 'Are you enjoying your first ever stay with us here at Gleneagles?' Somewhat taken aback by their knowledge of this, I began exuberating about what a wonderful time I was having. They then went on to wish me a lovely meal in the restaurant that I was booked into and concluded by assuring me that if I needed anything, they were there to help.

On top of making me feel like a very welcome guest, this brief encounter also put me at ease in an environment that, having not ever stayed in a place like it before, was out of my comfort zone. It certainly relaxed me and made me feel at home.

On returning to my room that evening, I saw that room service had tidied up. However, not only had they done all the usual stuff that I would have expected in a hotel of this standard – fluffing up the pillows, turning the bed down and leaving a mini selection box of chocolates on my pillow – they had also done something else. I didn't notice it until I was in bed, setting my alarm. They had moved the book I had been reading earlier on before going down to dinner, which I had left open, face down on my bed. They'd then placed it on my bedside table, having inserted a Gleneagles bookmark to mark the page I was on.

The next morning, I am half-awake and wandering down a long corridor in search of breakfast when an elderly looking gentleman who was busy hoovering turned his vacuum cleaner off, smiled at me and said 'Good morning, Mr Webster. How are you doing? Are you by any chance looking for breakfast?' I smiled and told him I was. He then escorted me to where it was being served, chatting to me along the way, asking me how I was and what I'd been up to so far during my stay. Now this well and truly knocked me off my feet!

Joining me for breakfast amongst a group of other delegates from the conference was the head of training for the hotel. I told him about the conversation I had had with the hotel receptionist and explained to him what an impression it had made on me. I always remember him saying, 'Adrian, we are a world-class five-star hotel; our whole focus is about making anyone staying with us feel incredibly special, to make each and every guest staying with us feel like they are the only guest we have. The person you are talking about is a professional receptionist, not only do they work incredibly hard at doing what they do so well, they also take immense pride in giving our guests the best experience possible'.

Having mentioned the lovely bookmark touch to him, I went on to enthuse about my encounter with the wonderful person I had just met on my way to breakfast, telling him of how impressed I was by him knowing my name. He response was 'Creating a welcoming atmosphere and delivering an exceptional experience is the collective responsibility of all of us in the Gleneagles team'.

I thought, wow, what a brilliant attitude! And then it struck me; if everyone adopted that same outlook and approach, how much better things could be for not only customers but also for employees everywhere. Having read recently that 89% of customers switch to a competitor following a poor experience, I really do struggle to understand why so many businesses and organisations – large and small, in both the private and public sectors – just don't seem to understand how much better they could be. They could be such amazing places to work in, and such fantastic places for customers to connect with, whilst at the same time being so much more successful. If only their people adopted that same, simple attitude. After all, as I keep banging on about it – TNTs cost nothing!

Surely, there can be no better fulfilling feeling than knowing you've helped brighten up someone's day and made them feel not only valued and appreciated, but a little bit special too. Seeing someone's face light up or hearing the delight in someone's voice down the other end of a phone or receiving a 'wow' message in response to a TNT that you've done for them – is both heartwarming and uplifting.

But that's enough of my experiences for the time being; I would now like to hand over to some of the many people who have taken the trouble to share their TNTs – sometimes as the recipient of a heartfelt gesture or an instance of outstanding service, and sometimes as someone who has taken an opportunity to give a TNT and, in doing so, touched or changed someone else's life. I am humbled by many of these stories, and I thank each and every one of these contributors for sharing their experience.

Old Friend

Some years ago, my wife Marlisa and I were in search of a traditional authentic Spanish tapas bar in London. She's Spanish and loves croquettes. London has many top-end, white linen, white glove restaurants. All of them I am sure are very good at what they do in terms of service excellence and the 'product' they deliver, but we were looking for something a bit different. A friend who lived on Park Lane told us of El Pirata on Down Street, one of those small Mayfair hidey holes that seemed to fit the bill.

On arrival, the restaurant was packed, the staff friendly and the atmosphere and ambience great. We were greeted like old friends, genuinely and warmly, even though we had never been there before, by a man called Roberto, who it turns out was an owner–manager. We were given a table near a service station and close to the open kitchen. Not ideal, but having booked late, and seeing dishes leaving the kitchens and smells entering our nostrils, we were excited. We had an amazing meal; the food and service exceeded our expectations and lived up to our first impressions. Roberto came over to ask if we had enjoyed our meals and to offer us coffees and deserts. Something caught his eye, and a look of horror was barely disguised behind his smile. It turns out that someone, somehow, had spilt oil, food juice or something similar on my blazer, which was hung over the back of my chair. I hadn't noticed it and certainly wouldn't have apportioned any fault or blame to Roberto or his excellent team. Ironically, they had offered to hang our coats up for us when we arrived, but I declined as I had my phone, wallet and various personal items in the pocket and felt better keeping the jacket with me. Roberto assumed that something must have been spilt on my jacket when a waiter had cleared our table or walked past to another table. He insisted on taking the jacket, taking my address, and having the jacket dry cleaned and delivered to me the next day. He also insisted on taking our wine and desert off the bill. He hadn't needed to mention the spill, let alone offer to help in such a gracious and generous fashion.

This took place 22 years ago. Roberto has since moved on, and his junior now runs the show. For many years, I have recommended El Pirata, taken countless clients there and had company Christmas parties at the place, so the pay back on this one simple act runs into tens of thousands of pounds in revenue. That's client service – at the cost of a bottle of wine and £22.50 for dry cleaning. The restaurant is now 'secretly' very well known and well frequented, and it's always busy. To this day, I can walk in and be remembered and treated like an old friend, even though I have been living in Cape Town for 15 years and probably only visited a handful of times these past few years.

Dino Cooper

We're Open

I am sharing this post from Ricky Webb, the general manager of one of our Marston's rotisserie pubs in Kent – The Star Sidcup Place, because I am so incredibly proud of the team there! If ever there was a shining example of going the extra mile and making a real difference by showing some empathy and compassion to those most in need in the community around us – this is it for me.

Dennis is a 96-year-old veteran who likes to visit us regularly. He also lives with dementia, and this can mean he makes the trip to see us outside of our opening hours. We sometimes find him peering through the window at 8 am thinking it's lunchtime and wondering why he can't get in . . . or coming in for his dinner at 10 pm after our kitchen has closed, believing it to be earlier than it is. We can only imagine the confusion he experiences day to day, so we do our little bit to try and make the confusion a little less. We welcome him at 8 am . . . sit him down and whip him up a quick brekkie and a warm cuppa . . . we seat him at his favourite table at 10 pm and let him know his dinner won't be long . . . little gestures from us that really do make a difference to him.

Sometimes you have to just take a moment from reading the 'good/bad' online reviews and look at the impact you have on the lives of people who won't broadcast it or review online . . . they simply let you know in person how you made a difference.

Dennis is special to us, and it warms our hearts to know he feels the same 🩶

According to a member of the team who has been at the pub for seven years, Dennis has been in for a meal every day during her time there.

Jo Bradford

Service with a Smile

The first few years of our son's life have been pretty fraught with a history of meningitis and subsequently a recurring petechiae (non-blanching) rash which appears when he's coming down with any virus. I have been advised that, whenever this rash presents itself, I should take him for blood tests, just to eliminate the worst.

Arriving one day to pick my daughter up from nursery, I noticed as I was lifting my son out of his car seat that the petechiae rash had returned and was starting to spread over his torso. Feeling anxious, I got to the nursery door and rang my friend who is a doctor. His advice was to go to A&E as soon as possible, but not to panic. My husband was 50 minutes away on the tube, and I now had a poorly 18-month-old son with a 3-year-old daughter in tow.

The people at my daughter's nursery were lovely and said that they would look after her for the afternoon, but asked if I would pick her up some lunch from the shop at the end of the road. I obliged, got to the door and realised that I had left my purse on the kitchen table! The teachers kindly gave me £20, but as I was getting out of the car at the busy Tesco Metro, my stress levels began to spiral as I realised that I must have dropped it. My son was crying in my arms and I just didn't know what to do, so I too began to cry.

Noticing my apparent distress, a man wearing a Tesco uniform (who was on a break outside the shop) came over and asked if I was okay. His gentle, kind and calming nature in that moment as I explained my predicament is something which I will always be grateful for. 'Come with me, I am the manager here and will get you all the shopping you need', he said. He then followed me around the shop with a basket whilst I got my daughter her lunch. As I was leaving, he asked me which hospital I was going to. As soon as I told him that it was one in Central London, he looked concerned. He knew from his own experience about the parking issues which I was soon to encounter, so he took a £20 note out of his wallet, put it in my hand and said, 'You will need this'.

After profusely thanking him, I assured him that either myself or my husband would be back the next day to pay for our shopping and pay him back his money. His parting words were said with a smile: 'I know you will'.

Emilie

TNT Thinking Smile with your eyes and listen with your eyes – the eyes have it. Besides being the simplest yet most powerful of TNTs, a nice smile is also the most infectious. Transcending all languages and instantly recognised in all cultures around the world as a positive affirmation of goodwill, a smile has no bounds. However, when people think of a lovely smile, they probably tend to think of someone flashing a beautiful set of perfectly formed, dazzling white teeth. The good news for those of you who are not natural smilers or those of us who have not been particularly blessed in the dental department is that you don't have to smile with your mouth. Instead, you can have the same positive and possibly more sincere effect simply by smiling with your eyes.

If smiling is the most powerful of human expressions, listening is by far the most important of all communication skills. One of the main problems with listening is that, when someone is talking to us, our ears don't give off any visible signal that we are actually listening; they don't start waggling or bleeping, nor is there a little tell-tale light that comes on. The only real way of indicating to someone that we are listening to them is by maintaining eye contact.

The next time you meet someone's eyes with a smile, you could be giving them a double TNT.

Hot Chocolate Inspiration

Today is day 128 at the Blackburn Royal.

I had been feeling off for a while and had a stomach condition called diverticulitis. I assumed it was that and took over-the-counter medication to try and deal with it.

I hadn't been able to sleep on my side for weeks, and one morning I managed it. I was asleep for maybe an hour when I heard and felt a popping sound. I'd never known pain like it and leapt out of bed.

I could feel fluid gushing in my stomach and knew it was serious. I called an ambulance, and the paramedics took one look at me and bundled me in the ambulance. I remember the ride there, remember arriving at hospital and remember them taking me out of the ambulance, and then I passed out. I was out for the next 32 days.

My intestines had split, so all the bad stuff that runs through them spilt out and was infecting my other organs. I was rushed into surgery where they were basically just trying to keep me alive, but they had to stop after six hours when I had a heart attack. My parents were told it was highly likely I wouldn't make it and to prepare for the worst.

I somehow got through it; but, after 48 hours, the sepsis I had caught was so bad that it was also going to kill me. My parents were told that the doctors had to try more surgery again but the chances were I wouldn't make it again. But the surgeons worked miracles, and I somehow managed to pull through.

I was on dialysis and a respirator, I had five lots of surgery that first week, but I made it. When I came to, I had lost the use of my legs and right arm. I'm learning to use them again, but none of that matters – I made it despite having next to no chance.

Being here for so long, you genuinely form relationships with people. I count some of them as friends now, including my lead consultant. I just don't have the words to explain the esteem in which I hold her. Put simply, I would not be here without her. I have two sons aged 6 and 11, and because of her I have the chance to still see them grow. I'll never be able to properly repay her.

My aim on Sunday is to walk down to Costa with my two sons and buy them a hot chocolate. I had mentioned this to a couple of nurses in passing.

Today my consultant slipped this on my table when she was doing her rounds.

She is incredible. I have no words.

Kevin Clarke

Good Service x 2

Whilst on holiday in New York, I purchased a unique new shirt but inadvertently left it in the hotel wardrobe when I came home.

I rang the Hilton in Times Square and told the receptionist what had happened; he said he would look into it for me.

Three days later, the shirt was couriered to my home in London with a compliment slip saying 'with our pleasure'. (No charge.)

I rang the hotel manager to thank them and requested him to personally thank the receptionist for his exceptional service.

A more recent TNT – I thought our integrated fridge was leaking water as the tiles were wet under it and across the kitchen floor. I ordered a new one and paid for it to be installed from Appliances Online.

Upon delivery, the installer said the old fridge was not leaking and traced the leak to another integrated appliance. He said you don't need a new fridge and called his firm, who agreed to a full refund. He then got a new hose for the other appliance and fixed the leak. I asked him how much I owed him he said 'nothing'. Obviously, I gave him a good tip.

What fantastic service.

Dave Fletcher

Favourite Room

Jurys Inn Hotel, Derby, 30 Oct 2019

I asked the receptionist at check-in if I could have the same room as last time.

Her reply blew me away: 'Certainly, sir. I've already reserved room 721 for you because I know you liked it so much last time.

I seem to remember you said it was in a really quiet corner of the hotel, so I thought you'd like it again this time'.

Holger Garden

TNT Thinking Ear tugging and pot plants. I was chatting to a lovely old gentleman who before retiring had been a concierge for many years at The Dorchester Hotel in London. He told me that one of his favourite tricks to help guests who were arriving by taxi feel a bit special was to welcome them as they got out of their cab and ask them if they had stayed there before. If they said yes, he would walk into the reception area behind them, carrying whatever luggage they had. Upon putting the luggage down, he would glance across at the receptionist, catch their eye and give one of his ears a couple of quick tugs! This was his signal to let them know that their guests had stayed with them before. The receptionist could then greet them by saying 'Welcome back to the Dorchester'.

I once related this story at a conference I was speaking at. Afterwards another ex-concierge came up to me and said that his way of letting reception know if a guest had stayed there previously was even simpler. 'If they were repeat guests, I used to put their suitcases down on the floor by the pot plant!'

Caring at Invicta Court Care Home

June's big day

During June's one-to-one, June and I discussed her wedding day. June presented me with a beautiful photo album that had a selection of images from her big day. We looked through the album together, with June pointing out to me who was who and what role they played on the day. June singled out one particular photograph and stated that it was her favourite of them all. She innocently mentioned that all of her wedding images were sadly in black and white and expressed it was such a shame as they somehow just didn't appear to truly represent what a wonderful day it was. This comment stuck with me, and I asked her if I could take a picture of her favourite photo from her wedding day and try and get it made into colour for her. With June's permission, we sat down and discussed in great detail what the colours in the picture were.

I managed to outsource an editor who was kindly able to transfer the colours that myself and June had discussed onto the image. Once they returned the image, I got it printed via a special photography lab to ensure a high-quality image and had it framed. Invicta Court's manager (the brilliant Jacqui Pompeus), team members and myself all presented June with her completed gift. June was overwhelmed and said upon first seeing the image,

'Oooo, that's lovely! I didn't think it would be in very much colour'. June was so pleased and has since been thanking me on a regular basis. Soon after receiving it, she had it placed on the wall directly in front of her and has since informed me she smiles at the image daily.

Becky Lyons

Madge's memories

Now 98 years of age, Madge was born in India as an Anglo-Indian, and she had six brothers and was the only girl. She grew up in India and often dips into those memories with fondness. During one of our conversations, she mentioned in passing how, in her late twenties, due to unrest in India, her family sought to send Madge and her elder brother Bernard to England in advance of the rest of her family coming here to seek a safe place to live. In India, they had a big house and servants, and when the family first all arrived here, they lived in one small room. It was a difficult time, especially for her dear mother.

Having told me the name of the ship they travelled on, I looked online to see if I could find any information about it. Having found some, I printed off an image of the ship and, along with a brief summary of her six-week adventure on board it and some brief details of its history, I had a picture made up for Madge.

Madge was very moved and excited to see the ship. So excited that it opened up all sorts of memories for her, and she chatted happily for days about it! She was so thrilled and kept a copy to show her husband and the rest of the family.

Jude Coveney

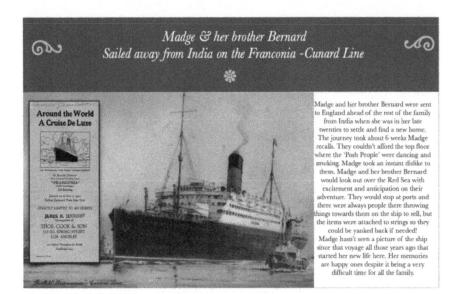

Madge & her brother Bernard
Sailed away from India on the Franconia -Cunard Line

Around the World
A Cruise De Luxe

Madge and her brother Bernard were sent to England ahead of the rest of the family from India when she was in her late twenties to settle and find a new home. The journey took about 6 weeks Madge recalls. They couldn't afford the top floor where the 'Posh People' were dancing and smoking. Madge took an instant dislike to them. Madge and her brother Bernard would look out over the Red Sea with excitement and anticipation on their adventure. They would stop at ports and there were always people there throwing things towards them on the ship to sell, but the items were attached to strings so they could be yanked back if needed! Madge hasn't seen a picture of the ship since that voyage all those years ago that started her new life here. Her memories are happy ones despite it being a very difficult time for all the family.

The RMS *Franconia* was an ocean liner operated by the Cunard Line from 1922 to 1956. She was second of three liners named *Franconia* that served the Cunard Line, the others being RMS *Franconia* built in 1910 and the third *Franconia* in 1963. She was launched on 21 October 1922 at the John Brown & Co shipyard in Clydebank, Scotland. Her maiden voyage was between Liverpool and New York in June 1923; she was employed on this route in the summer months until World War II. In the winter, she was used on world cruises.

Wartime service
In September 1939, she was requisitioned as a troopship after refitting at Liverpool. She had a collision off Malta with a French troop ship called the *Marietta Pacha* and was escorted to Malta by the armed merchant cruiser *Alcantara*, but was repaired in time to take part in the Norwegian campaign. On 16 June 1940, while en route to St Nazaire as part of Operation Ariel (the evacuation of the Second British Expeditionary Force from France), she was damaged by near-misses from German bombs and was escorted back to Liverpool for repairs.

Later in the war, she took troops to India and took part in landings at Madagascar, North Africa, Italy and the Azores. In 1945, she was used as a headquarters ship for Winston Churchill and the British delegation at the Yalta Conference. At the end of the war in Europe, *Franconia* made several trips across the Atlantic carrying returning US troops and refugees. After VJ Day, she was employed repatriating British troops, including freed prisoners of war from India. During her government service, she had covered 319784 miles (514642 km) and carried 189239 military personnel.

Legacy

Franconia's pre-war around-the-world cruises and distinguished wartime service made her a popular name within Cunard. Hence, in 1963, RMS *Ivernia* was renamed *Franconia* to continue the name within the company. In recognition of her important Canadian immigration role, Cunard Line gave the builder's model of *Franconia* to the Maritime Museum of the Atlantic in Halifax, Nova Scotia.

Growing Customers

A client gave my colleagues a very nice tip on completion of an extremely challenging landscape garden project. They were surprised and delighted by his unexpected generosity but not so much as I was when his wife brought out a gift-wrapped box for me. When I got home and opened it, I was humbled to see a limited-edition bottle of Scotch (my favourite tipple) beneath the wrapping paper!

A few weeks later, we were asked by my client to price another job at his son's house. He was nearly as happy as I was when, after completion, I told him it was on us.

These TNTs can be a perpetual gift. My client has since booked me in for two other projects. It goes to show that TNTs are hugely important.

Gary Bashford

Happy Shoppers

When I worked at Safeway, we used to wipe dry the shopping trolley seats whenever it rained, so that the child sitting in it wouldn't get a wet bottom, and the whole shopping experience would be a far happier one for the parent pushing the trolley!

Gordon MacDonald

Out of the Hat

I needed a dress shirt and bowtie for the office Christmas dinner and, as a busy family man with two kids, I had only one shot at it; Saturday afternoon in Camberley – no pressure!

So, accompanied by my wife, 10-year-old son and 2½-year-old daughter, I braved the high street on a Christmas shopping Saturday with much trepidation and not much idea where to start, not being too familiar with the mens' fashion retailers in town.

After very short visits to two shops, the kids' patience and mine were wearing thin. On the promise of a 'drink and cake after this shop', I dived into Moss Bros, leaving the wife to distract the kids with a wander around a 'plastic tat shop'.

I had barely found a shirt that I liked and was about to try a sample on for size when the family materialised, prompting an urgency to finalise my purchase that I wasn't anticipating.

And this is when the store manager pulled out a TNT.

He found my daughter a top hat from the Wedding Hire section and showed her the mirror. She was so happy wandering around the shop all dressed up, stopping at the mirror for a quick check every now and then.

As for my son, well he was given a jacket to try on and the tie rack to peruse. And after that, he was offered made-to-measure cloth samples to play 'Match suit materials with liners' – who thought that game could be such fun!

So, with my children fully occupied, the pressure was off, and I was given the time, space and freedom not only to find a shirt and bowtie for the Christmas party, but also a lovely new suit which my wardrobe had been crying out for, for years.

And thanks to the manager and his TNT, I will be going back.

And the family got their drink and cake!

Alan

Salt 'n' Pepper

One of our drivers was making a delivery to a construction site in Derby, where he had offloaded the goods and was seeking a signature for the POD.

He walked into the site manager's cabin, where he was met with a rather unhappy individual who was staring at his microwavable macaroni cheese. 'Everything ok?', the driver asked, 'it's just, I could ... umm ... do with a signature'. 'NO' grunted the individual, 'some thieving bastard has taken my salt and pepper'. Our driver eventually obtained a signature and climbed back into his van.

Then, this particular driver did what he does best – he went the extra mile. With his brain whirring, he darted across the road to a TK Maxx store and purchased, out of his own money, a salt-and-pepper grinder set from the kitchenware section. He then popped back onto the worksite and poked his head around the door of the cabin that he had just left, only to be greeted with a 'What now?!'

'Umm, I just went and got these for you', he said as he presented the site manager with the salt-and-pepper gift.

The manager put his knife and fork down and lifted his head, and an unending smile appeared on his face. This was followed by a stream of thank you's and words of appreciation.

That manager continues to be a good customer to this day.

Adrian Fowler

Pterodactyl Postal Service

I will never forget the customer service I received from Odeon Cinemas. It was at a time when *Minions* and *Jurassic World* were the main films showing.

As a nice treat, my partner booked the cinema tickets online as it's usually me that would sort it. We remembered why I sort it when we realised he had booked the tickets for in five minutes time instead of in a few days. We were at home in Pjs and would never have made the showing.

We emailed Odeon, explaining the situation, and received a prompt reply from a lovely customer service assistant advising that it was no problem, and that they would send out a credit note that we could use to repurchase the tickets for when we wanted them. The credit note was general so the following wasn't required, but regardless of that, the customer service assistant personalised her response and asked if it was *Minions* or *Jurassic World* we were hoping to see, before confirming the tickets would be sent to us via pterodactyl. We were delighted that they were sorting the issue for us after it was our mistake, and the response made us laugh.

To our delight, when the credit note came through the post, it was accompanied by a little picture of a pterodactyl!

It was such a small and simple personal touch that made a big impact on us, and I'm always telling people about it.

Natasha Greene

Fender Surprise

For some time, I've wanted a Fender Blues Junior amplifier in a Tweed cabinet, and I found one listed on musicstore.de, a German music website.

I ordered it thinking I would need to replace the power lead with a UK three-pin plug. Imagine my delight on unwrapping my delivery to find 'UK Plug Adaptor – no charge' listed on the invoice.

This little act of thoughtfulness has ensured these guys are now my favourite online store for music equipment.

If they are this nice when I didn't ask for something, I can imagine they would try really hard if I ever had a problem with anything I ordered.

Stuart Holah

Saw You Coming

See a customer heading towards the store from a distance?

Start their usual latte, so it's ready when they arrive.

Oh, and throw in the odd free cookie to thank them for their custom.

It's what we always do at Subway Silverburn, Glasgow!

Abid Sadiq

What, No Macaroons!

Gave blood for the 50th time recently, taken by the same nurse as previously. The last time, I had joked about there being no macaroons anymore, and she had said she'd make sure they were reinstated for my 50th – but they weren't. I jokingly said I was mortified.

When I went for my cuppa afterwards, she popped out to Waitrose next door and bought me a giant macaroon out of her own pocket.

I was of course thrilled, so much so that I related it back to the head of the transfusion service – who gave her an award.

Mike Ward

Pumped Up

I got in my car today to find my low-tyre-pressure warning light illuminated. On checking the tyre visually, it was not fully inflated, so I drove to my local tyre replacement store.

As I entered Tyre City in Northwich, I was greeted by the manager, who asked me to drive my car into the repair bay. Two young men immediately removed the tyre, checked it, found a nail, took it out and repaired the puncture.

I thanked them. I went back to reception delighted that I had not had to purchase a new tyre. I asked the manger for my repair bill, and he said, 'Oh don't worry, you are a customer of ours, we have done it free of charge, stay safe'.

That's how you respond to the Covid-19 pandemic – with professionalism and great customer care.

I shall always buy our tyres from this store and recommend them highly.

Thank you.

Roy Newey

Singing Conductor

I have a big smile on my face, right now, in this moment, ignited by the conductor on my 7.01 commute to Waterloo.

A few quotes as he walked up the coach:

'Sorry to trouble you lovely people at such an early hour, but if I could take a quick glance at your tickets, that would be wonderful'.

Starts singing.

'Can't beat a bit of Frank Sinatra . . . show me your tickets or the singing starts up again'.

Big chuckle.

'Good morning madam, that's a lovely bright ticket pouch you have on you there, lovely colour, suits you'.

She's beaming.

The whole coach is smiling. It really only takes that, a bit of joy and human interaction.

Imagine what today would feel like if we all made a conscious decision to turn up the dial on joy and being human, even by just 10%.

Today is going to be amazing.

Sally Earnshaw

Many Happy Returns

I run a venue in Birmingham which is part of a bigger organisation called Flight Club Darts. We are a food and beverage business, but our USP is our darts – pretty awesome even if I say so myself!

One of our best TNTs that we use very successfully is as follows:

> When someone makes a booking to come and play darts, as part of the booking process, we ask if it's for a special occasion, as quite frequently it's to celebrate someone's birthday. This being the case, we make a note on the system to remind us when the guest comes in. Then on the day while they are playing, we prepare a nice little chocolate brownie for them, dress it with a special candle, grab a birthday card with a voucher in it, and as one big team we stroll over to the oche together. We then all sing from the top of our voices a very happy birthday to the lucky person.

This little unexpected gesture always gets a warm response. More often than not, you can hear the surprise and joy in the person's voice, along with a little embarrassment I might add, and a lot of laughter!

All in all, a great TNT that always hits the spot.

Frank Burden

TNT Thinking Laughing is good for your health, no joke!

As well as being a magnet for drawing people together, laughter is a medicine that is freely available to all. When you laugh, you increase your own intake of oxygen-rich air, which stimulates your heart and muscles. At the same time, endorphins get released, your mood gets a boost, your anxiety levels tumble and your all-round feel-good factor rockets. Some studies have shown that having a good laugh can bolster your immune system, thereby increasing your chances of being around a bit longer.

Memorable Appointment

I love a good TNT experience. I went to an osteopath last year, and, during my first appointment, he asked me a few non-osteo-related things about my life throughout the session. Without me knowing, he jotted a couple of things down about our discussions at the end of the session.

So then, for my second appointment, he referred back to his notes and asked me things from our previous discussion months prior, such as 'Did you end up finishing your kitchen project?' and 'Did you carry on watching *Love Island*?' It made the experience much more personal and really memorable.

Remembering things about others makes them feel important in the time they spend with you, especially when they know you are someone who sees many clients in a day. It's the little things that count.

Lucy Goffin

Bon Voyage

In April 2010, I was fortunate enough to have taken a transatlantic crossing with my sister on Cunard Line's *Queen Mary 2*, sailing from New York. We had a great time and were treated very well; everything was lovely.

We were lucky enough to repeat the experience in January 2012. We entered the ship, where there was an assortment of staff waiting to greet each and every passenger in person. This was only the second time we had ever sailed with them. We were greeted by several people in the same way, a large smile, and told 'Hello, it's nice to have you back'. This was repeated several times throughout the crossing as we met different crew members that we had met previously. Priceless!

We took our 12-year-old niece on the second trip. She had been through a rough year, with her mum having been in and out of hospital, but even at 12 she recognised what good service looked like. We had taken her to New York for New Year, spent five days there and stayed at the Waldorf Astoria. Her best bit, however, was her time on the ship. There are several things that made her trip memorable, all centred around being made to feel special. The crew had no idea what had been going on in her life, but it didn't matter – this is what they do.

This is a ship that has 2500 passengers at any one time, and it was 20 months between our visits. As for me, I would sail with them in a heartbeat, and hope to do so again next year.

Sarah Burns

Out-of-Way Recognition

In my experience as a Buildbase showroom manager in Barnsley, it's always the little things that go a long way. Despite the heavy snow falling outside, a very happy customer came in to see me with these. I love my job!

Colin Day

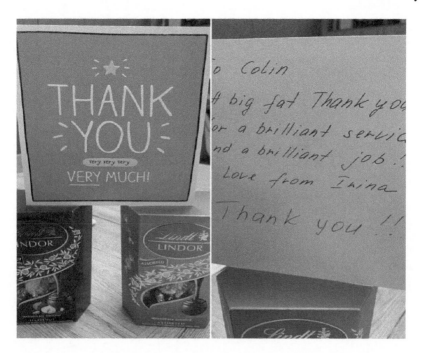

Understated

When our kids were eight and six, respectively, we went on a family holiday to Austria, where we stayed at the Aqua Dome Hotel & Therme in Längenfeld. During our stay there, we experienced a stunning mix of low-key, but high-impact service.

For example, each day, the drinks in the room fridge would be replaced. On day 1, the kids drank the two mini bottles of blackcurrant juice. On day 2, the hotel restocked the fridge with four bottles of blackcurrant, which of course got used. By day 3, the other juice flavours had been removed, the top shelf of the fridge was full of blackcurrant juice bottles, and there was a hand-written note from housekeeping saying that we should call if we needed any other flavours returned.

The other memorable service touch was a letter from the hotel manager waiting on our doormat when we got back to the UK, thanking us for staying at the hotel.

Needless to say, we returned to that hotel a few times over the years, and hope to again.

Dr AJM, Kent

Hear to Help

My sisters and I went to visit our grandmother, who had been in hospital for five weeks. We visited her regularly, and it was the highlight of her day to see our faces and listen to what we'd be doing. At the ripe old age of 99, her hearing wasn't what it used to be. She wore hearing aids, one of which had unfortunately been lost in the hospital, but she just about managed to hear with the remaining one.

On this particular visit, we noticed she wasn't hearing well at all, so we took out the hearing aid and saw that a wire had become dislodged.

We asked the hospital staff if there was anything they could do.

They advised us that there was an audiologist across the road in a separate building. It was around 12 noon, so we hurried over, hoping it hadn't closed for lunch.

When we arrived, there was a lady in the reception; we explained the situation and asked if they could help. The lady said in a stern voice and not-so-friendly manner that we needed an appointment and that the audiologist was about to finish in the next few minutes and wouldn't be returning until the following week.

I'm not sure if my sisters and I looked like we were about to start crying, but the lady suddenly said 'Give me a moment'. She went away and returned a few minutes later, saying 'The audiologist will see you now'. Absolutely gobsmacked, we hurried in, thinking we'd need to be quick as we knew he'd officially finished for the day. I don't know what she had said to him, but not only did he take time to talk to us, he went and mended it and gave us some free batteries too. Boom!

As we were leaving, we went to thank her for getting the audiologist to see us.

She took our hands, smiled and said, 'I could see in your eyes the love you have for your gran and how special she is to you all'. With that, she gave us a wink, God-blessed us and wished our gran a speedy recovery.

My sisters and I could not believe our luck that day and will never forget the love and kindness projected. Both the lady and the audiologist truly demonstrated exceptional TNTs. Our gran, Dorothy Littlewood (Granny Bear) sadly passed away on 8th May 2018, falling short of reaching her 100th birthday.

Lisa Gledhill

Why TNTs go BOOM! A boom sound from a TNT occurs when a person goes way beyond someone else's expectations. It is similar in many ways to the noise created from the shockwaves of an object passing through air faster than the speed of sound. TNTs exploding, just like sonic booms, generate enormous amounts of energy, resulting in a relatively much smaller but perfectly audible thunderclap between the ears.

To understand how this happens, I'd like to take a quick look from my perspective at the human mind. There are only three things we need to know when it comes to TNTs and booms. First, our minds are split into two, the conscious and a much bigger subconscious. Second, our minds don't speak any language, they work in pictures. Third, between the conscious and subconscious, there is a filter to block and prevent us overloading our minds with big stuff – we can only take onboard the big things once we have had time to step away, reflect back and digest them. In other words, when we have broken them down into lots of little manageable bits.

Unlike big things, TNTs being so small are able to penetrate straight through this protective filter and gain split-second access to the subconscious, where they detonate on impact, creating a huge, instantaneous, explosive picture. This immediate 'hit' triggers a sudden surge of emotions, top of the list being that of surprise, the number one favourite emotion of your subconscious's oldest resident, a now wide awake and highly excited inner child.

'BOOM!'

Belated Birthday

We arrived in the early afternoon for an eagerly awaited overnight stay at the Four Seasons Hotel at Trinity Square, London. It was a 50th birthday present for me that unfortunately had had to be postponed due to Covid-19 and my husband Larry's shielding.

On arrival, a lovely man at the reception asked me if we were there for a special occasion, and I said that it was a very late birthday present. On arriving back at our room that evening, having enjoyed a fabulous dinner together, we found this lovely personalised card wishing me a happy belated birthday, along with some chocolate bon bons. A small thing, but it made me feel very special.

Maggie Banda

Food for Thought

I was in Foodland, my local supermarket here in Adelaide, looking for some Pecorino cheese. The lady at the deli counter helped me out and presented me with a chunk of cheese. At the same time, she asked if I would like her to grate it for me – no charge, all part of the service.

I was blown away. The number of fingertips I have lost grating cheese for pasta!! Lesson learnt: This is about delighting the customer with the service you deliver and being proud of what you do.

Justin Porter

TNT Fact Classical music being played in wine stores inspires shoppers to buy more expensive wines.

Feeling Blessed

Wow – what a lovely birthday surprise from Nikos Kokolakis, his family and staff at Kokalas Resort, Georgioupolis, Crete.
Thank you!

Lena Edberg

Beyond Our Remit

I work at Lanyon Bowdler (LB), a leading UK law firm, and I once had a client whose husband, a maintenance engineer, had died following an accident at work. I was instructed by my client in respect of a fatal accident claim for loss of financial and services dependency. Her husband had always managed their computer, and after his passing, she could receive emails but was unable to send, and she was getting upset by this. I asked our IT department to assist. They set her up with a new Gmail account, and she was quickly up and running. This was outside of our mainstream service, but it helped build a really good relationship with the client.

I have subsequently introduced the last item on the agenda for our Personal Injury Department meeting as Notable Achievements and TNTs. It's a great way of giving recognition for going the extra mile.

Another example: we had a client who was really anxious about an examination by a psychiatrist for an expert report. Without the report, we couldn't progress the case for her. She had failed to attend appointments twice despite lots of encouragement. On the third occasion, her lawyer Karen Clarke picked her up, took her to the appointment, all the while reassuring her – and then dropped her off home. The client was delighted.

Our managing partner Brian Evans does a Happy Mondays email every week highlighting this sort of thing.

Neil Lorimer

Bulb Blowing

I was staying at the Jumeirah Emirates Towers hotel in Dubai shortly after it opened, about 17 years ago. I'd been amazed by the attentiveness and service of the staff throughout my short stay there, but one moment blew my mind.

We'd left the room to go out for the day, but I realised I'd forgotten something (I think probably cigarettes!) and went back to get whatever it was.

As I went back to the room, a maintenance guy was up a ladder changing a light bulb, the smartest looking guy I've ever seen up a ladder – wearing a suit. As I went to walk past him, he climbed down, moved the ladder and simply said, 'Please excuse me, Mr Cook'.

I said, 'Oh, don't worry about it, no bother', got my stuff and went out. He waited until I'd passed and wished me a good day as he got back up the ladder.

To this day, I don't know how he knew my name, but I've never forgotten how impressed I was.

Adam Cook

Back Down the Pub

I used to work for an American firm, and my office was in High Holborn looking down Chancery Lane. I worked there for around 10 years, and trained there to qualify as a trade mark attorney. We had a great sociable department, and it was often the case (usually two or three times a week) that some of us would go for a drink on the way home. Our favourite pub was (and still is) The Mitre in Ely Place, a short walk from our offices. There was a great barman there called John – silver haired, and always friendly. I think he had been with the pub for some years. He got to know our group.

Eventually the office closed. I worked for a time at the parent of the UK company in Swindon, commuting back and forth. The group of us who used to gather in the pub are still in touch, and indeed I usually have a few days' holiday with one of them each year on the UK canals.

After moving away from the American firm, I worked for a pharmaceutical company, and then a telecom company, both in London, but remained in touch with the various contacts from my original US company.

Some years after our London office closed, probably 3 years, we all met up again and went to The Mitre. Imagine my surprise when we walked in to see John behind the bar as usual.

He said, 'Hello Maggie, are you still travelling to Swindon?' It really made my day!

Maggie Ramage

TNT Thinking Using someone's first name. Some say that a person's first name is the most important word to that person, I have no doubt that this is probably correct in the vast majority of cases. What is absolutely certain in all instances is that a person's name is the strongest connection to their own individual identity, and using it is the best way of getting their attention.

When we remember someone's name having only just met them, or when we reconnect with a person whom we've only ever encountered on rare occasions before, and we use their name – in addition to showing respect and making a good impression, it also makes them feel that they are important to us, that having bothered to remember it, we must genuinely care about them.

Using someone's first name in a conversation also tends to soften the interaction, making it less formal and more intimate. Often when politicians are on the ropes whilst being grilled by a persistent interviewer, they will resort to calling them by their first name in an attempt to sweeten their interrogator.

Remembering people's names and using them effectively is something that I've noticed over the years a lot of highly successful people go out of their way to do. It's a powerful TNT that leaves a lasting impression and is one that regularly gets raised during discussions in workshops I'm running.

Problems Owned

On my last flight out of Vienna on a budget airline, we were horribly late. Having spent hours hemmed in together at the boarding area, we finally boarded the plane and sat waiting to take off for what seemed like an eternity, but in reality was probably around 40 mins. It was the end of a long day, and we were all tired. Eventually we took off, landing at Gatwick at something like 1 am. As we taxied along the runway, the captain gave the standard 'thank you for flying, etc. and 'sorry we're late'. We docked, the seat belt lights went out, we started to leave the plane, and when I got to the exit, the captain was standing there, personally apologising to every passenger for the delay, wishing us a safe journey. . . None of it was his fault, but he took responsibility.

A young lady working for a car hire company at Heathrow is presented with a customer who is clearly distressed, upset and fretting. He is German, and needs to get home quickly as he has just been informed that his wife has been taken seriously ill. His plane has just been cancelled until the following day, and his plan is to hire a car so that he can drive through the night to his hometown. However, the hire terms do not allow you to take a hire car out of the UK, so she could not offer him a car. The man is in pieces. The young lady asks the man to wait a moment, and she disappears into the office. She comes back after a while and says, 'I've looked at the airline schedules, and there is a plane to your city from Gatwick. It leaves at x. I've looked at the coach transfer times, and you will not get there in time to catch the flight. . . but I've spoken with my manager and I can take one of our cars and drive you to Gatwick'. Which they do, and the man catches his plane.

It seems such a simple thing in hindsight, but we read this in the young lady's CV when she applied for a job with us, and it pretty much got her the job! One fairly large act of random kindness!

Andy H

All okay?

I checked into a hotel after a long train journey to London from Leeds. It was late, I was tired and I had lots of client meetings the next day. I get to my room, put my suitcase down, when suddenly I get a call on the room's phone. I pick it up, and it's the front desk that I'd just checked in at, asking if I'm okay, if the room is okay and if there's anything I need. I have never had that before, and that tiny phone call made my whole night.

Charlotte Mather

TNT Thinking The benefits of asking.

I've always regarded question marks as being like little Velcro hooks that enable us to connect with people.

By simply asking a few questions, we are not only showing an interest in someone and opening them up by getting them chatting, we are gaining a better understanding of their particular needs, thereby best placing us to be ready and prepared to go beyond their expectations with TNTs that really do hit the mark and mean a lot to them.

Whenever possible, I think it's always impactful to end a customer interaction with an 'anything else?' question, or a 'happy ending' question as it is sometimes known. It gives them a reassuring feeling that they are in safe hands and that we are there for them, no matter what their needs.

TNT Fact Studies show that a four-year-old child on average asks 437 questions a day. 'I didn't realise it was so few!' is probably what any parent of a four-year-old reading this right now is thinking.

Merritt Christmas

I took my family to New York in April 2019. This week, I got a Christmas card from TUI Cowley Centre. Not unusual, except this has a stamp on it and was handwritten with a message in it. Real care and thought, I felt remembered. They retain my custom.

James Merritt

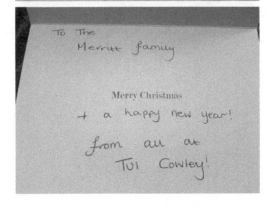

Scottish Hospitality

My personal TNT memory from Gleneagles: not only did the staff recognise my wife, Susan, and I, but they also warmly welcomed our French Bulldog Poppy by name every time she visited. Poppy loved the place and the attention too!

Another TNT from a bastion of Scottish hospitality is the Loch Lomond Golf Club, where your golf bags are taken to the first tee and picked up from the last green and returned to your car. The locker room team polish your shoes when you're on the golf course and polish your golf shoes when you're in the 19th hole having a beer after your round – you feel very privileged indeed.

And a third TNT from yet another great Scottish institution. Not sure if they still do this but The Three Chimneys Restaurant in Skye used to have a policy where they would open any bottle of wine on the wine list to pour you a single glass – and only charge for a glass!

Keith Mitchell

No Problem

I had a meeting planned in Birmingham with a lady I haven't seen in eons to reconnect and discuss business, and she had booked a restaurant called Opus in the business district. Nice summer menu and all that.

Table booked for 12 noon, so I promptly arrive at 11.55 am – only to see the chefs all walking out of the restaurant and down the road, followed by everyone else. The fire alarm had gone off just at the moment the restaurant was due to open for lunch.

I stood outside like a lemon with my bags and paraphernalia that one needs when on the road for the week, obviously looking a little lost. My colleague arrived, and that is when the most delightful TNT occurred.

The owner of the restaurant came straight over and apologised. Rather than give us a sob story or the hard sell about how we should wait out the fire alarm, she picked up my bag (very heavy) and marched us over the road to her competitor, spoke to the manager and bought us both a glass of champagne to apologise.

Nothing more, nothing less – just good-old-fashioned hospitality.

Of course, we could have stayed where we were for lunch – but guess what? An hour later, and perhaps slightly tiddly, we went back to Opus and had lunch.

Her kind actions made a really memorable day and delivered an emotional connection that I will not forget.

Karen Turton

TNT Thinking Take ownership of problems and spin them into TNT opportunities. When striving to deliver a terrific customer experience, there is no better golden opportunity to blow the socks off customers with some cracking TNTs than when one of them has a problem. It is your chance to shine through your mistakes, demonstrate the level of service you can deliver and, most importantly, show just how much you care. Never simply apologise to a customer and rectify the problem – instead, swing into action and sweep them away with a solution that surpasses anything they would have ever imagined. Problems are pregnant with TNT opportunities. Whenever anyone has a problem, that problem always gives birth to a need – and a need needs a solution!

Whenever I overhear a customer making a complaint and, to my amazement, hear a member of staff start arguing with them, coming up with some pathetic excuse or even trying in some instances to persuade them that there isn't actually a problem, I despair. Arguing with a customer, let alone trying to get them to think that they don't have a problem, is not only insulting a customer's intelligence, it's commercial suicide – it's madness.

You may well win the battle and save some money on the day, but you will not only lose a customer for life, that unhappy ex-customer will go around telling anyone who will listen about what an awful experience they had.

Something I witnessed one particularly warm afternoon a few years ago when I was on stage delivering the after-lunch slot, speaking to an audience of approximately 300 people, has always stood out vividly in my mind. The room was absolutely baking hot, delegates were desperately fanning themselves with their conference brochures and I was melting while presenting on stage under all the lights! It was blindingly obvious to everyone that the air conditioning had packed up. When I'd finished speaking, the organisers called for a member of the hotel management team to come and fix the problem during the coffee break.

When a manager eventually turned up, instead of apologising and setting about taking steps to resolve the issue, they immediately adopted a confrontational stance and went on the defence by stating, in a somewhat aggressive tone, that they had already checked if the air con was working and that, in their opinion, the room wasn't too hot at all – 'not for this particular room'. My ears couldn't believe what they were hearing! Then, having refused to even acknowledge there was a problem, let alone accept any responsibility or even be seen to make any attempt to do anything about it, they strutted off in a huff. The managing director of the company who's conference it was turned to me with a look of astonishment on their face and said, 'We've used this venue for the past three years. Never again!'

A pinch of sugar goes a lot further than a fist full of salt.

– Annie Webster

On the other side of the coin, I was talking about this particular experience to a lady I'd met at a conference, and in response she started telling me about a charismatic entrepreneurial hotel owner she once worked for who used to deliberately create the odd little problem here and there for guests, so that he could be seen to go out of his way to fix them!

Special Requirements

When I booked into the Ibis hotel, George Square, Glasgow, I'd forgotten that under the 'additional requests', I'd asked for vegan snacks. Got to my room and discovered these little reminders!

Harry Webster

Two-Way Street

We both do a lot of travelling. When we do receive really great service, we always make a note of the names of those responsible. Then, after returning home to Canada, we contact the most senior people that we possibly can within their company. We describe the experience we had, let them know just what a positive difference those individuals made, and explain why, through their TNT actions, they have motivated us to return. A lot of people are quick to complain, but few take the time to say 'thank you'!

Natalie and Francois Boyko

> **TNT Thinking** If people have given you a great experience, tell them! Recent surveys show that consumers are 21% more likely to leave a review after a negative experience than a positive one. It takes just a few minutes to go online and let someone know what a great job they're doing and to let them know just how good they've made you feel. It not only makes them feel over the moon, it inspires them to go and do it for others. If they've made your day, go make theirs!

Ice Cream Craving

It sounds stupid but . . . at the time I was a stressed-out student doing a food shop at about 9 pm on a Friday night. In my stressed mid-exams state, I desperately wanted chocolate ice cream. Nothing fancy, just the regular own-brand cheap stuff. I went and asked a staff member who was unpacking in the frozen section if he knew where it was. He looked at me strangely, checked his cage and then vanished.

I was fairly confused until he reappeared two minutes later with a tub of ice cream for me! He had gone out and found it in the stock room and brought it out for me. I could have cried, because he had just done something so sweet for me when he didn't really have to. He could easily have said 'Sorry, it's not out on the shop floor right now' – but he went out of his way to help me and, even though it was so small, it meant so much at the time.

Just for clarification, I was completely sober at the time. Most people would need a couple of drinks to get emotional over ice cream, but not me!

Vici Hemming

Happy Ever After

When we were coming back from honeymoon in Mexico, we had issues checking in online for our flight home, which meant we had to do it at the airport. This meant that my wife and I couldn't sit next to each other but in separate rows on the flight home. Needless to say, a bit of a blow and sore point after a great two weeks away.

Anyway, when we boarded the plane, one stewardess did everything she could to find us seats together – but to no avail, as the flight was fully booked and not a single spare seat was available. A really nice touch that she even tried.

The 9–10-hour flight passes and, just after we land in the UK, the same stewardess comes to me and apologises for the flight home, knows it isn't a great way to end a honeymoon, gives us a bottle of wine and passes on her congratulations to us both! Boom!

A situation that she could have easily walked away from and not returned to – but went out of her way to make a memorable impression – which needless to say she achieved.

Matt Holdstock

. . . And Relax!

For my 19th birthday, my boyfriend bought me a voucher for the two of us to visit The Shard in London. As we walked towards the entrance to this imposing building, I suddenly felt nervous and underdressed. What if my sundress and trainers, or my boyfriend's shorts, were too casual? What if our online voucher wasn't valid?

The man at the reception desk looked up. 'Hi guys', he said. 'Are you here to visit the observation platform?' I hesitated and fumbled with the creased voucher.

The receptionist cracked a huge smile. 'I see you have a voucher, which is great. I need to take that off you, and point out where the lift is. I'd also like to welcome you to The Shard – you can relax, now that you're here. Just so you know what to expect, there are two restaurant bars on the observation levels, and the upper one is usually quieter if the lower one is busy or you just want some space. Take as long as you want, enjoy the views and, most important of all, have a great time'.

And, just like that, I realised all my nervousness had disappeared. Was the receptionist a mind reader, or was this his welcome for everyone? What I do know is that he made the difference and ensured we had a relaxed experience that we will remember forever.

Izzy, Exeter

TNT Thinking Experts estimate that we have up to 80,000 thoughts a day, 80% of which are negative and 95% are repetitive. What this tells me is that there must be an awful lot of people out there feeling far more anxious on the inside than what they appear to be on the outside. I know that whenever I'm feeling concerned about something, it always seems like everyone else is happily sailing along without a care in the world – how wrong I must be! Appearances can be extremely deceptive, and I think it is important to recognise that, despite giving the impression that they are positively brimming over with confidence, what's going on inside someone's head may well be a very different story.

Knowing this, any TNT actions we take to help drive the stress out of a situation and put someone's mind at ease, no matter how small those actions may be, are likely to have a much bigger effect than we may well think or ever know. As Robin Williams once said, 'Everyone you meet is fighting a battle you know nothing about. Be kind. Always'.

I think it is especially important to remember this when looking after new customers or new starters in a team. You may have grown used to the environment you are working in and become familiar with who's who and what's what. To an outsider or a newcomer, however, things can be quite daunting and all a bit overwhelming at first, when everything is completely new to them, and well outside their comfort zone. The tiniest of TNT gestures – a smile, a nod of the head and a few warm words – is all it usually takes to make them feel at home and how they are feeling on the inside to start matching their appearance on the outside.

Whilst I'm on the subject of taking away people's anxiety, one of the most common negative TNTs that I hear mentioned time and time again is when someone rings someone with a problem and that person, having promised to ring them back with an answer, doesn't. Not knowing what's going on, if anything is actually being done about it, is something that really does begin to wind up those who are normally the calmest and most placid of people. As I used to repeatedly say to all my team, 'Always ring people back, even if it's just to tell them that you've got nothing to tell them!'

2

Team

During coffee breaks at conferences, delegates often tell me why they love their job and wouldn't want to work anywhere else, or they whisper in my ear that they are thinking of leaving. Either way, the motivation behind their thinking is never down to one particular reason that they can put their finger on; it's always to do with an accumulative 'cocktail' of TNTs.

People may go home and moan to their partners about TNT incidents that have wound them up that day, but they probably won't mention them at work for fear of them being seen as too petty or trivial. As a leader wanting to retain good people, I was always acutely aware of this; I was forever listening out for the things that people weren't telling me. I was also conscious of the fact that not everyone thinks like I do.

As a motivational speaker, when I'm at social functions, I sometimes get approached by people who, having found out what I do for a living, are eager to share with me their secret for motivating people. It's great that they have an interest in the subject, and I'm delighted for them that they have found the secret, because I certainly haven't! I really don't believe there is a secret to motivating people – but, having said that, I do know there are a few 'keys'.

When you consider that, in one workplace, there could be up to five different generations of people, all thinking and working differently, along with four fundamentally different types of personalities – and all from diverse backgrounds, the chances of guessing what motivates someone is like guessing the lottery numbers. We are all, thank goodness, completely different, and we are all motivated by different things.

From my experience, the first key to inspiring people with TNTs is a very simple one – it is to not only recognise and accept but to actually proactively celebrate the fact that we are all different. If we are to have any hope of inspiring all our people and getting them collaborating and pulling together as one team, it is vital that we always bear in mind that a TNT that floats one person's boat isn't necessarily going to float everyone else's.

The second key is that, before we can even begin to motivate anyone, we first of all have to somehow engage with them. If we want to stand any chance of doing this, we are going to have to listen to them and try and understand where they're coming from and, probably more importantly, where they'd like to go.

In one of the workshops I run, I ask people what it is they want more than anything else from those around them in their team. We always end up with a sea of multicoloured Post-it notes all over the walls with words such as 'recognition', 'support', 'empathy', 'respect', 'validation', etc., on them. No matter what team they are in or wherever in the world they are from, or for that matter whoever they are, all these words percolate down into the same three words at the end of each session: 'time', 'care' and 'human'.

If we want to connect with each other and help each other grow, no matter how crazily busy it may seem or how hectic it may feel, we have to make time to talk, even if it's just for a few short seconds. When we give people our time, we are sharing our most precious commodity. One thing I've noticed about all truly great leaders is that, no matter how much they have on their plates or what pressure they are under, they always manage to find time and make space to be with – and talk to – their people. When managers tell me that they just don't have the time that they need to engage with their people, I ask them how long it takes for them to say 'How are you, how's it going?'

Moving on to the second word, 'care' – we have to show on the outside just how much we care on the inside. I don't mind working long hours, commuting into work, doing a tough job, dealing at times with some difficult people and giving it my all, so long as I think people around me care. That they care not just about themselves but also about the rest of us in the team, about our customers, about our services and about what we are all striving to achieve. I think one of the main issues here is that a lot of people probably do genuinely care, and they assume that everyone around them knows that they do, but unless they are able to demonstrate it now and then with just the smallest of TNT gestures, people may well get the impression that they don't.

The third word, and for me the most interesting one, is 'human'. Like me, most people I talk to want to work with authentic people who are not infallible, who now and then make mistakes. I am always thankful for having people around me who are able to laugh at themselves, let go and have some fun. I really do struggle to connect with anyone trying to portray themselves as being perfect. By all means, go in pursuit of excellence, and please do strive at all times to be the best at whatever it is you do, but please don't ever try to come across as perfect – it's the biggest turn off there is. It's probably always worth remembering the old joke about why they put rubbers on pencils and bumpers on cars – because we all make mistakes!

I personally would much prefer to be disliked for who I am rather than be liked for some pretend person that I'm not, and I really wouldn't want to be part of a group where anyone felt they couldn't be themselves – that they had to be continuously on their guard, acting out a role, never letting their mask slip.

The truth is that we can't force someone to engage with us, but we can begin to connect more with each other through a few TNT actions, such as giving up some of our time and putting an arm around others when most needed. Hopefully, by doing this whilst at the same time being more open about a few of our own imperfections, we can all work together to create a transparent environment where everybody feels comfortable in their own skin – a place where everyone has the freedom to become the best possible version of themselves.

As a business, you will only ever be outstanding if you make your customers feel outstanding, and this will only have any hope of happening if the people in your teams feel outstanding. If they feel great about themselves and the roles they play, chances are your customers will feel great. It is the base camp starting point for any successful organisation, large or small.

I always remember being at a dinner party many years ago. Sitting around the table was a group of people from an eclectic collection of professional backgrounds, including law, finance and medicine. Hosting the evening was a retired couple, both of whom, if my memory serves me right, had previously been senior partners in a law firm. Seated next to me was a very affable man named Bill, who I'd never met previously. Suddenly, from across the other side of the table, Bill got asked a question by one of the hosts, 'What do you do, Bill?' Bill replied with considerable pride in his voice, 'I'm a salesman'. An awkward, prolonged silence fell around the room before eventually his wife interjected with 'Oh, but he did used to be a teacher!' The silence, along with a few disdainful looks and his wife's obvious embarrassment didn't, however, seem deter Bill in the slightest, as he went on to wax lyrical about how much he loved being in sales.

With Bill's attitude and that of the people in the Gleneagles team that I talked about earlier constantly in the back of my mind, it crushes me when having asked someone what they do as part of a team, they start their self-description with 'I'm just. . .'

It really does make me want to grab hold of them and shake them! I want them to realise that no one should ever see them-selves as an 'I'm just', and that if that is how they do actually view themselves, it is unlikely they are ever going to begin to enjoy the fulfilment of making a difference for others. I think one of the main reasons why the level of customer experience we are all invariably exposed to is so mediocre these days is that there are far too many people in customer-facing roles who regard what they do as merely being something of a stop gap, until they find a 'proper job'. I want people in a team to have the same obvious level of pride in whatever they do as Bill and develop the same refreshing, positive outlook that I witnessed at Gleneagles.

The bottom line is this: if we are to get the TNTs spot on with our customers and blow the competition away, everyone must feel passionate about what they do. I most certainly wouldn't ever want any 'I'm just' or 'stop gap' people in my team. If people felt like that, I would honestly feel, as a leader, that I'm not doing a very good job, that I'm letting those who feel like that down, and that both the culture and the environment that I am responsible for are failing. When it comes to acting together to deliver TNTs, I think it is crucial that an environment be created and maintained that not only engages and retains people but also positively encourages people to want to continuously keep on learning, developing and progressing together. At the core of that environment, I'd like to see a culture that shouts out to its people that they can make a difference, no matter what they bring to the table – no matter what their job title is, or whatever anyone else may think!

My mantra has always been: 'Nobody is a nobody, everyone is somebody, we all have something to give – let's go make a difference together'.

The only time you should look down at someone, is when you are helping them up.

– Jesse Jackson

Take a Break

I took over the IT team here at Norgine earlier in the year, and I'm really keen to build a family culture within the team.

So, one TNT idea I had was around our bi-annual survey, notified via email, where each employee is asked to complete a series of questions. However, we all receive a huge number of e-mails daily, and it's really easy for these to get missed.

What I did was ensure that all our IT team members received a handwritten note on their desks attached to a KitKat, thanking them for their work and asking them to 'take a break' and complete the survey (called VOICES).

I ensured this was done in all our offices across Germany, France and the UK. We ended up with 100% completion rate on the survey, and people still talk about it today.

Marc Gorham

Starfish Difference

Some years ago, I was a Special Constable for Watford Police, and a big part of my role was focused on the nighttime economy and policing football games. Completely unexpectedly, our Chief Superintendent sent me a small starfish pin after a minibus driver from Huddersfield wrote a letter to thank me for treating the visiting fans with respect and for taking the time to welcome and support them rather than being faceless. This felt like a double TNT from the driver and the senior officer, the starfish symbolising Loren Eiseley's famous story 'The Star Thrower' – about how anyone can make a difference.

What I loved about the ethos in Hertfordshire police, as you will see from the letters I received, is that we treated our citizens as customers to serve and had the same customer service mentality you might expect to see in the retail world – focused on being human and realising that how you make someone feel will stay with them for the rest of their life and may indeed shape their entire view of the whole institution of policing. We even had a long mirror at the rear exit door to the station with a sign to remind us when going out on the streets that how we presented ourselves to the public would be the first and perhaps only opinion they would have of us.

Moving forward to the present day and where I now work – having learnt such invaluable lessons from my time with the police, I am always consciously aware of how the little things we do can make such a positive difference and boost the feelings of those most in need. I have recently seen an increase in colleagues opening up about mental health challenges, especially in our younger talent, and I'm actually reassured that even young men are now open to talk. I have a small thing I do with individuals who've opened up to me. We agree on just one emoji and, if they ever send that emoji, I know without any further discussion that they need to talk.

Lindsey Rowe (Glennie)

Date:	30TH September 2014
Our ref:	
Contact name:	Chief Superintendent Bill Jephson
Direct line:	

Dear Lindsey,

Everyone Can Make A Difference!

I am very pleased to write to you to thank you for your assistance given to John Beaumont from J.R.T. when he attended a football match at Watford on 3rd May 2014. He thanks you for ensuring he could park his minibus safely and easily find it after the match had finished. He was very impressed by the professionalism and respect all officers showed. John has been left with a very positive impression of Hertfordshire Constabulary following your actions.

I would like to take this opportunity to present you with your very own 'starfish' as a reminder that you really have 'made a difference'. Because of your helpful, sympathetic and caring approach you have earned the gratitude of a very satisfied member of the public.

I hope that you feel proud to be able to provide members of our communities with a quality service and the "personal touch" that can so easily bring reassurance and support. I certainly feel very honoured to be in command of a team of individuals who are valued by the public they serve. When I receive letters of appreciation I am reminded of the commitment, skill, dedication and care you, and others like you, show to members of the public every day, often when they are at their most vulnerable.

There is no greater praise than that of a very grateful stranger who may never forget what you have done for them and the impact you have had on their lives. Never underestimate the impact of your actions and be sure to make the most of these opportunities because they build public confidence, respect and much needed support.

Well done and thank you.

Bill Jephson
Chief Superintendent
LPC Commander

Local Policing Command
Hatfield Police Station Comet Way, Hatfield, Herts AL10 9SJ

'Reducing Crime, Catching Criminals, Keeping People Safe'

www.herts.police.uk

Chief Constable

23 June 2014

SC Lindsey Glennie

Local Policing Command
Watford Central Police Station

Dear Lindsey

Please find attached a copy of a letter I have received from John Beaumont expressing his appreciation for the professionalism, intelligence and respect shown in assisting the transportation of supporters to and from the Watford ground on 3 May 2014.

I would also like to personally pass on my thanks. Appreciation such as this is always satisfying to receive and reflects well on you and the Constabulary as a whole.

Yours sincerely

Andy Bliss QPM
Chief Constable

You've been Mugged!

We've recently introduced a new TNT initiative at school, to thank staff for going above and beyond, and to make them feel special and acknowledged for doing so.

It involves staff members being presented with a unique mug, emblazoned with the words 'I've been mugged at Five Acre Wood' and our #TogetherStronger logo.

The person presenting them with the mug fills it with a range of handpicked 'goodies' such as hot chocolate sachets, sweets, etc. The following week, the recipient then decides who they would like to 'mug', again awarding a colleague a mug filled with selected treats.

We have purchased 500 mugs, with the intention that all staff will at some point have the honour of being 'mugged', as well as the privilege of 'mugging' someone else at work!!

Staff are already proudly showcasing their mugs; they will hopefully create a lasting impression, as well as further enhance our sense of team spirit, and the well-being of staff.

FAWS – Senior Leadership Team

TNT Thinking Dare to do things differently. If you are to differentiate yourself with imaginative TNTs, you will have to be prepared at times to completely screw up!

Whenever you try and do anything that's radically different you will always attract criticism. If you want to stand out from the crowd you will have to be brave enough to step outside, stand on the front doorstep of your comfort zone, and stare failure in the face. Getting it wrong now and then is the only way any of us ever learn, excel, and deliver knockout TNTs.

Fear knocked at the door. Faith answered. There was no one there.

– Martin Luther King Jr

Paul's Tree

We lost our much-loved colleague and friend Paul Atkinson this June to a brain tumour. We wanted something permanent to remember Paul by. A few suggestions were spoken about – a bench with a plaque on it, plants around the office, and a tree were just a few of many options considered. In the end, we thought a tree would be the best and most fitting tribute for Paul, as it would be permanently visible for all to see whenever they came to our offices here at UK Power Networks.

It was decided that a cherry tree would be the perfect tree to plant, not too big, yet colourful in the spring. Planted in the right location, it would be clearly seen from our break out break-out room as well as appreciated by those eating their lunches or enjoying some quiet time whilst sitting on the benches outside. It would be a wonderful reminder of Paul.

I emailed Nancy, Paul's wife to tell her of our plan, and she thought this was a very kind idea. I spoke to Tom, Paul's brother, who also works for the company, and he too agreed that this would be a really good way to remember Paul.

I rang ALS, our groundworks contractor, and they agreed to donate and plant the tree free of charge. After agreeing this with the principal tenant of the building, we arranged a date for the planting of Paul's tree. ALS turned up the day before to make the ground ready for the planting the next day.

On the day of the planting (18th September 2020), the two ground workers from ALS were a little nervous, as they knew they would have a big audience when putting the tree in the ground and backfilling it. I went to see them that morning and prepared them by stating 'You have never been under so much scrutiny for planting a tree!' They took this comment in the jokey manner it was meant. At 2 pm, around 50 people gathered outside where the tree was to be planted. I asked everyone to bring face coverings as we couldn't have fitted everyone in the space and maintained social distancing. Fortunately, everyone got to see the tree being planted. It was especially good to see Nancy there, chatting with Paul's colleagues. I opened up the tree planting by thanking everyone for coming and making a joke about not seeing so many people for such a long time (due to COVID-19).

I handed over to Martin McCrae, who was very close to Paul and saw Paul as his best friend. Martin did a great job at giving a 10-minute remembrance speech and finished off by quoting some one-word descriptions he had of Paul from Paul's colleagues. While Martin was speaking, the tree was being planted, and by the time the speech finished, the tree was in place, Martin asked everyone to take a few minutes to remember Paul and played some of Paul's favourite music from the Rolling Stones in the background. Once everyone had taken the time to quietly remember Paul, they started to speak with each other and talk about the good times they all had with him.

The tree planting isn't quite finished, and we are going to site a stone set at the base of the tree. Paid for by generous contributions from all the members of staff, it will be in the colours of Paul's beloved Maidstone United, with a picture of Paul and the words 'For Paul, a colleague and friend'.

James Cooper

From the Top

One TNT stands out for me.

Twelve years ago, I was asked to host/compere the HSBC Training Department Christmas Conference. It was a good day enjoyed by all.

The following week, I received, through the post at home, a handwritten note from the Head of Learning. It was written using a proper ink pen, just a dozen words to say a personal 'thank you'.

I still have the note somewhere. It meant so much as they'd taken the time to do that rather than send an email or pass a message via the several managerial layers that sat in between us.

Dave Barry

My Cuppa Tea

I came back from my training camp last month, which was abroad and consisted of lots of bike riding – so, in effect, a Redford dream holiday! On my first day back, my boss Kathy Clarke gave me a present in appreciation of the little things that I do at work and to welcome me back.

It was a really thoughtful present, combining my love of tea, my dog and the great outdoors. It definitely counts as a TNT, and it put a spring in my step for the rest of the week.

The gift was a personalised mug with me and my dog overlooking a beautiful lake with the mountains in the background. It is now my favourite and makes me smile and reflect on having a fantastic boss every time I use it.

Jerry Redford

Yours Forever

When I started out as a teacher, I was fortunate enough to join an amazing school, with a truly inspirational and pioneering headteacher. The school was based on the other side of the country from my home area, and the headteacher took me under his wings from day one, He treated me like a son.

I had no money, so he gave me an immediate advance on my salary (out of his own pocket), and refused any attempts I subsequently made to repay this (I still haven't managed to!).

I had an old, clapped out car which had to be scrapped, so he allowed me to 'look after' one of the school minibuses on a full-time basis. It became, to all intents and purposes, my company vehicle – to such an extent that when I somehow managed to get a city centre parking ticket one weekend, my headteacher personally footed the bill, and I wasn't recriminated in any way.

I didn't have a washing machine in my flat, so I was given the freedom to use the school washing machines. (This backfired at one point, but that's another story!)

In a day and age of ever-tightening budgets, he not only persuaded me that it was in my best interests to engage in master's-level study, but also ensured that I was fully sponsored over a four-year period.

There were so, so many other TNTs along the way; it goes without saying that the headteacher became so much more than my 'boss' – he was a friend, mentor, coach, counsellor, advisor and way beyond!

In return, he (and the school) had my absolute, undivided loyalty and commitment – I genuinely would have gone to war for him! But for the reorganisation of schools within the said local authority, and his retirement, I have absolutely no doubt that I would still be working with him.

Some 15 years on, we remain in close contact, and I still harbour the very same sense of loyalty and commitment.

Tim

Pit Stops

One of our simplest team engagement initiatives at JW Lees is an envelope on the wall for the team to write Post-it notes of thanks to each other.

The person with the most or most significant gets an hour off – or a 'Pit Stop', as we call it.

Whilst I didn't win (never expect to!), reading the comments this morning brightened up my very wet morning!

Thanks to Adrian for the idea.

Nicola Waring

As I am going away for a wedding this weekend and need to leave a bit early for some last-minute bridesmaid tasks, I was excited to be awarded a Pit Stop at our team meeting last week. It is great to know that my hard work has been recognised by my team, and the comments on their nominations about me were really lovely!

Here is a picture of our fabulous Pit Stop trophy, created by Nicola Waring's brilliant daughter. That's me in the driver's seat!

Helena Raymonde

TNT Thinking Money isn't the only motivator. When it came to inspiring teams on tight budgets, I needed to be constantly coming up with creative ways of keeping everyone connected and pulling together as one team. The key to me doing this was to give everybody a sense of belonging. When working in a large team, especially a team based in multiple locations, it is difficult at times to fully appreciate the work that others do. With everybody being so busy concentrating on what they are doing, all they ever get are fairly limited insights into what the rest of the team are up to.

In an attempt to draw people together, keep them hooked up and appreciative of others, I started employing peer recognition whenever possible. What I quickly discovered was that, if you want to give someone a sense of belonging, and, at the same time, motivate them through the roof, a personal TNT 'thank you' gift of recognition from their teammates works very well.

What I mean by 'personal' is something that may be inexpensive but has some real thought behind it and is meaningful to them, rather than something more generic such as a box of chocolates or a bunch of flowers. For example, new cycling gloves for someone who cycles to work, where it's been noticed that they could probably do with some warmer ones, especially with winter approaching.

No matter who they are, or how small it is, if it's a gift from their colleagues and it holds some special significance, it's pretty much guaranteed that the recipient will have a grin on their face for the rest of the week.

If, however, you are looking for a one-size-fits-all way of showing collective appreciation, you may want to consider rewarding your people with Pit Stops, as I am absolutely delighted to see JW Lees are doing!

Thanks to my wife Louise, Pit Stops are – by light-years – the most popular team 'thank you' that I have ever come up with.

Louise loved her job in London and, after many years of doing it, had long since got used to the commuting. One day, she happened to mention that the only real downside to the long hours she was putting in was not being able to just have an hour or two off during the week to, as she put it, 'catch up with myself'. With no spare time Monday to Friday, by the time she had recovered from the previous week and prepared for the next, there was precious little time for much else. Her passing comment gave me the idea of awarding Pit Stops.

A Pit Stop is an hour off work, voted for by non-management team members and awarded to other team members, including managers. At the end of each day, I used to invite people to vote for whoever in the team they thought had taken the biggest extra step that day for someone else, whether it was for someone in their team, someone else in the company or a customer. Those awarded them could either use them for the occasional hour off now and then or, in some cases, save them up until eventually they had eight in their 'Pit Stop bank', in which case they could take a day off – with eight being the maximum number of Pit Stops they were allowed to use up in one go.

Not having the financial resources I would like to have had at the time, it forced me to become extremely resourceful – in this instance, by rewarding my people with time. It made me acutely aware of just how powerful peer recognition can be; it also made me realise that there are other ways to motivate people without spending money. I have never seen people get so buzzed up and excited about going the extra mile as they are when it comes to winning a Pit Stop!

Many Hands

I have recently moved from London to LA with my organisation to open up an office and build a sales team from scratch. A once-in-a-lifetime opportunity, but equally the most outside my comfort zone I have ever been.

In my third week, I was quoted $1,300 to move from my temporary to my permanent accommodation.

My team all drove into the office at 7 am and asked me to cancel the delivery. After work, they all showed up at mine, filled their cars up with boxes and helped me move apartment.

It took some of them 2 hours to get home.

What an amazing gesture and TNT – something I'll never forget.

Tom Love

Caffeine Start

I'd moved into the head of culture role at ADNOC, and it was only my second day with my team. I arrived at my desk to discover a welcoming cup of coffee waiting for me.

No one ever said who did it, which makes it even nicer in a way as it felt like it was from the entire team.

And that, as a TNT on day two . . . means there is hope :)

James Vincent

Happy Anniversary

A TNT that sticks out in my mind happened in 2011. My wife and I were celebrating an anniversary and booked a trip to the USA, initially staying at a very nice hotel in Las Vegas. Within a few minutes of our checking in, a member of the hotel staff delivered a bottle of champagne.

I thought, 'My word, this is amazing service', before realising it was from the CEO and MD of Spicerhaart, the company I worked for, thanking me for my work contributions and wishing us both an enjoyable holiday.

I was really impressed by this TNT and have never forgotten that they took time out to make our arrival just a little bit special.

Steve Sparrow

IF YOU WANT TO GROW YOUR BUSI-
NESS, START BY MAKING YOUR PEOPLE
FEEL TALLER

Welcome

The week before I started with my new company, Benenden Health, I received a 'welcome to the team' greeting card which was signed by all my new colleagues.

It blew me away. I was beaming from ear to ear when I read it.

Mel Fletcher

Studies Paid Off

A previous employer of mine, Solectron Global Services, put me through a master's degree. A couple years after completing this, I left for a senior role with another company.

Under Solectron's 'Learning & Development' policy, I was due to pay back nearly 50% of this significant funding. My employer stated I had done enough for the company, waived the fee and gave me their best wishes.

Andrew Addiscott

Small Thing, Big Smile

I bought him lunch. No big deal.

He thanked me for lunch.

Then, I wrote the following message on a card and left it on his desk:

'I'm so impressed with your consistent positive attitude and work rate. We're really privileged to have you on the team. Thank you'.

Later, I saw a huge smile on his face.

He turned to me and mouthed the words 'thank you'.

People want to feel valued and their work appreciated.

It's not all about pay raises, bonuses and benefits.

Sometimes it may be something as simple as lunch and a small message of appreciation.

A person who feels valued and appreciated will always do more than what's expected.

Mani Ramasamy

TNT Idea If you want to show your appreciation to someone, be seen to go out of your way to do it. If you do it whilst just happening to be passing by, your words will be diluted and have a much lesser impact.

Royal TNT

My Royal TNT dates back to 2007 and the Formation Parade of the Mercian Regiment at Tamworth Castle in Staffordshire.

The Colonel-in-Chief, HRH The Prince of Wales, was there. After the march past and ceremonial stuff, Prince Charles was carefully taken from group to group to do the 'engagement' piece. In my group were two elderly veterans.

When Prince Charles got to them, looking both of them in the eyes, he said 'We've met before, haven't we?' At which point, both of the elderly gentlemen's faces lit up and they replied in unison, 'Yes, your Royal Highness, you came and spoke to us both when you visited Exeter in 1979 – we were bandsmen back then'.

Jeremy Redford

TNT Tip: Set aside ten minutes each day to chat to a different person.

Bowled Over

Whilst at HSBC, I worked for a wonderful boss, Dave Fletcher. Prior to Dave becoming my manager, I had, despite being a non-drinker, become used to receiving gifts of champagne or wine in recognition of performance. Then one day I received a gift that I will never forget.

I was at my son's cricket club watching him play when, completely unexpectedly, Dave, knowing of my passion for the game, turned up and presented me with a pair of cricket cufflinks as a 'thank you' for all my hard work. As a person who is mad about all things cricket, this TNT gesture meant the world to me.

Prash Thakrar

Dziękuję Ci

I sent all my general managers a bottle of champagne in January to celebrate a great Xmas performance and put a personal message on each bottle. I had a Polish couple working for me, and I wrote theirs in Polish . . . they were so grateful that I had taken the time and effort and thought about them.

I received so much loyalty afterwards. It's the little personal things that make the difference.

Will Porter

TNT Thinking What people see is what people see.

I was asked to go and speak to the entire workforce of a large engineering company. The reason I had been invited along was because, in the words of the managing director, motivation was at an all-time low, moral was on the floor, productivity was falling and even the most loyal employees were considering leaving. In the morning, I stood in the middle of a factory floor speaking to approximately 400 people, most of whom were machine operatives, warehouse staff and supervisors, along with a contingent of office staff, managers and directors.

When I'd finished my talk, there must have been at least a dozen or so employees who came up to me saying, 'We'll give you a TNT; they've taken away our biscuits!' It turned out that they used to have biscuits provided free of charge in their restrooms, but recently, due to cost cutting, this 'perk' had been taken away.

I could see real, genuine upset in their eyes as they vented their anger at 'the management' taking their break-time treats away, and I got it. It may seem like such a trivial thing to an outsider, but if I was working hard, doing a hands-on job and putting in long shifts in the same building all day – having become accustomed to enjoying a biscuit with my cup of tea or coffee in my break, that free biscuit would probably be something that I looked forward to. Having got used to it and then having it taken away – that would be a big deal.

In the afternoon, I was invited 'upstairs' to speak in the boardroom to their senior leadership team about inspirational leadership and to discuss ways of re-engaging their people.

Sitting around the boardroom table directly above the factory floor, the topic of conversation moved on to what TNTs they could start putting to good use in an attempt to start reconnecting with their shop floor. I told them about the complaints I had heard about the biscuits and pointed out to them what a demotivating effect this action appeared to be having.

The finance director responded by saying, 'Do you know how much those biscuits were costing us?!' I found myself glancing around the room at all the top-of-the-range, super-comfy-looking chairs. Each one of them had the appearance that they'd come with a hefty price tag. I looked at the FD and, as respectfully as I possibly could, I asked if I could offer them some advice. 'The next time you are buying office furniture, instead of buying these top-of-the-range-looking chairs, get the next best, and keep the biscuits. The biscuits are what the people who matter the most to this business see, and it's the cost of their absence that you probably need to consider'.

Fortunately, the FD took my advice in the way it was intended, and, from my understanding, the biscuits, to the joy of many, were reinstated. I think it's always worth remembering, especially as a leader, that no matter how hard, how dedicated or how committed you are, or, for that matter, how much work you may take home with you in your head – your people only ever tend to get snapshots of you. It's not often that they get to see the bigger picture as to what you're all about, how hard you work and how much you care about them. The snapshot pictures that they do have of you in their minds are incredibly important because they determine how they feel. They are TNT pictures that gradually add up, pictures of you that they take away and keep, pictures based on your actions or inactions. Vivid, enduring images. That's why a quick 'Hello, how are you?' really matters, and it's why seemingly miniscule things such as biscuits can be so consequential. Never overlook the TNTs – they're the big things to someone else.

With Love

I had a Valentine's Day TNT idea to send all of my ATG-IT staff who were not in London an individual valentine card along with a single red rose and the following message:

'Thank you for all of your hard work over the last year – even though we are not in the office today, we are still thinking of you'.

These were then placed on their desks by 8 am, ready for when they arrived at work. As you can imagine, that went down well.

Mark Matthews

Highflyer

Back in 1998, I had recently started my career as an engineer in one of the MOD research agencies. My boss was contacted by an RAF wing commander from part of the MOD procurement organisation, requesting support in developing some specifications for a new aircraft project. I was tasked with another new graduate named Bob to undertake this short task over a few weeks. It involved having several meetings with the wing commander, during which he gave us lots of supporting information and was generally very pleasant and encouraging, despite our relative inexperience.

Once our report had been reviewed and approved by our chain of command, and submitted to the customer, my boss received a very positive letter in response, thanking him for allowing Bob and I the time to produce such a thorough and professional report.

The fact that such a busy officer had taken the time to write this letter made us feel really appreciated, it boosted our confidence, and incidentally it helped our individual annual performance appraisals.

About nine years later, having moved into the procurement section of the MOD, I found myself joining a team of about 80, for whom the aforementioned wing commander was now the 1* air commodore. In this role, the air commodore had a way of making everyone, along with their individual contributions, feel highly valued. After a couple of years on the team, a colleague and I organised a sponsored long-distance cycle ride for some of the team. Having completed the ride and raised a not-insignificant sum for charity, we were surprised and pleased to receive individual handwritten letters from the boss to thank us for our efforts in devoting our personal time to run such a well-received event.

Again, the fact that such a busy officer, running a multi-hundred-million-pound project, had taken the time to appreciate our efforts in such a way made him stand out as a very personable leader and boosted our morale and desire to do our best for him.

Fast forward another five years, and I was seconded to a Department of Defense project office in the US. I was asked to support the 3* US Navy vice admiral who ran the project in a video conference with a British 2* air vice marshal on a topic I no longer recall. I discovered shortly before the call that the British officer was the same person referred to in the aforementioned two incidents of this story. As the admiral concluded his initial greeting, the air vice marshal thanked him for taking the time to participate in the call. Then, spotting me almost off the screen to one side, and bearing in mind I was at that time sporting a full beard and a somewhat unmilitary haircut, he broke off to say 'I'm intrigued by the rather hairy looking officer to your right. Is that (my name) by any chance?' He then asked how I was and how my family were all doing, before returning to the subject of the call with the admiral.

The fact that he remembered me and acknowledged this in such a high-powered environment really marked him out to me as a leader whom people would willingly follow anywhere, because he had the ability to make you feel important as an individual, and he personally appreciated one's contribution.

These three examples are, in their own right, singularly important TNTs, but the consistent application of TNTs as the officer rose through the ranks makes him, in my mind, a truly great leader.

Al

From Fran

I work as a teaching assistant in a local infant school. My teacher had been off on long-term sick leave – on her return, she gave me this amazing 'thank you' note which blew me away. It really meant a lot.

Andrea

To Andrea,

Where do I start. Thank you so much for everything you've done. I really don't know how to thank you enough. When I found out in the Summer that you would be my TA I was truly over the moon and just couldn't wait to start working with you. I have loved every minute so far and all I wanted was for you to have the best year. I'm sorry that it went a little wrong but I know Jane would have been amazing. I can't wait to get back to normal and enjoy many years working with you as it's the happiest I've been at work in such a long time. You're truly one in a million and so lucky to call you my TA and the children don't know how lucky they are.

Love you lots

xx Fran xx

TNT Thinking The importance of saying 'thank you'. Saying 'thank you' is one of the easiest ways to nurture relationships. When we say these simple words, we are not only acknowledging what someone has done for us, we are also letting them know that they matter to us.

If you were only allowed one TNT to exhibit how much you care, saying 'thank you' each and every time someone does something for you would have the most effect on you and those around you.

Seasonal Thoughts

When I joined my company at the start of Easter, they gave everyone a personalised Easter Egg from Thorntons with their name on it. Such a little thing, but pretty cool. At the moment, any parent working in the business receives an Amazon voucher for Christmas.

Craig Dalziel

Father–Daughter Inspiration

Wrote my daughter a note telling her how proud I was of the work she was putting into her A-level revision and left it with her bag this morning.

Got an 'I love you' message when she left for school.

Now to put it into practise at work #TNTs

Craig Leverington

Mine's a 99

We, The Ice Co., are the UK's No. 1 ice brand. Although year-round sales are growing, we are still very seasonal. A spike in temperature or a heatwave can bring huge peaks in demand, along with added pressures on the team to get stock manufactured, distributed and into the nation's largest supermarkets for people to buy and enjoy.

Last summer, during a particularly hot heatwave, the owners of the business decided to reward all employees with a spontaneous ice cream van!

It was a massive hit with employees and is spoken about to this day.

Ginny Durdy

Hugs Online

The buzzer went – it was an Amazon delivery. I'd not ordered anything. It was a small book titled, '100 Hugs, a little book of comfort' with a gift note from a colleague: 'Sometimes you just need a hug from a friend. Clearly, I'm not there, but here's a little book of hugs instead xxx'

Oli Burbage-Hall

Feeling Appreciated

Today, I received this right at the end of the day from a colleague of mine, Caprice Dewhurst. It made everything all worthwhile!

Katie Warren

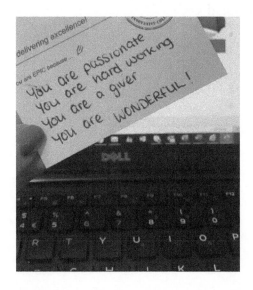

TNT Thinking Listen out for 'pocket powers'. I have always found that a good way to help create more of a close-knit family culture is by constantly acknowledging and highlighting the personal attributes that people bring to work, on top of the skills that they are being paid to bring – their 'pocket powers', as I call them.

I wouldn't ever want anybody in my team to feel like they are merely two-dimensional, that they are only defined by their job title and limited in what they can bring to work by what it says they do in their job description. I want them to know that they can bring so much more, and that all of us in the team value the difference that those additional things make – whether they bring energy, empathy, humour, passion, optimism, clarity, experience or maybe a calming influence – whatever it is they have to offer.

Caring Bosses

My first boss in the recruitment sector, Robert Walters, paid personally for me to have a serious shoulder operation at a specialist unit in Harrow. It needed to be done quickly, and he facilitated this and allowed me the 12 weeks post-op rehab without any employer pressure.

When at Harrison Willis, my second child was born. After a few months, she was seriously ill, and my MD Graham Palfrey Smith and his wife offered to drive from London to Herefordshire to pick my son up and have him whilst my wife and I spent time in hospital with Katherine. A fantastic thing for a colleague to offer.

Stuart Blake

Sincere Thanks

I opened my work inbox this morning to see an email from a colleague, whom I admire a lot, personally thanking me for a project I'd recently completed. It wasn't just a 'yeah, thanks' kind of email; she'd put a lot of time into setting out exactly what she was thanking me for. This TNT (tiny noticeable thing) put a spring in my step.

Lyndsay Cartwright

At Home

The main aim of our cultural change programme at Linc Cymru Housing Association is for all our staff to feel connected to the business and its future.

We have taken three simple TNT steps to help achieve this:

Dress for your day: This approach was based on giving responsibility back to colleagues to consider their day ahead, the business outcome desired and what they would wear to achieve it. It was based on one of our new values: 'Respectful'. *Dress for your day* is as much about me showing respect to colleagues to allow them to relax into their day and empower them to make the right decision, as it is about them considering who they are going to meet that day and respecting their requirements. It had an immediate impact, with the office feeling more relaxed and people showing more of their personality. Customers have also commented that visits feel less like a landlord–tenant relationship.

Kick-starting your day the right way: It is important to us not to overlook the little things that make people feel at home in work. Providing free tea and coffee in this instance was already in place, but we wanted to give people more of a choice. So, we set up premium-brand-tasting sessions. Quite simply, the one that runs out the quickest is the winner and reordered for the future. It's now called 'the posh coffee'.

Becoming frail doesn't mean life stops: Applying our business purpose – 'creating the right environment for people to flourish' – is of the utmost importance to us in our three nursing homes. Residents moving through each phase of their lives should be able to benefit from the enjoyment that more independent people take for granted. Having listened to residents and their relatives, care staff took it upon themselves to create a bar to enhance their social life. Besides helping recreate memories, it's become a focal point for families and residents. It has gone down extremely well, especially when Wales are playing rugby!

Scott Sanders

Kosta's Coffee Mug

On my first day at Reed in Partnership as head of leadership and management development, the 'Learning and Development' team presented me with my own coffee mug inscribed with a gold 'K'.

I knew from that moment that I had made an awesome choice for the next stage of my career.

Kosta Christofi

Sent Home

At The Brunts Academy, Mansfield, we don't leave 'thank you' cards in staff trays, we post them to their home address so that having landed on their doormat, they come as a nice surprise for the recipient.

Our CEO, Claire-Marie Cuthbert, writes personal letters to every member of staff.

Natalie Aveyard

For Everyone

We had a sales director named David Garden.

Dave was great for TNTs because large corporates like ours drive people hard, and the small personal steps that he used to take for everyone made a very big difference. For example, he would always make a point of verbally highlighting outstanding achievements, simply by taking a moment on drive time to call and say 'well done'.

Beyond that, it would not be uncommon for a care basket full of fine wine, cheese, crackers and biscuits to arrive for myself and my entire team when we achieved our milestones. Small, unexpected gestures of recognition these may be, but it is these explosive TNTs that make it all worthwhile.

Let's just say the personal note David sent me along with one of the packages is still up on my office wall! Did I really care about the wine and cheese? Not really, but his thoughtful acts stuck with me. Additionally, he did not send a gift just to me, but to everyone on my team who had helped achieve targets.

Chris Gearren

Family Business

When my son Charlie was born, my then boss at HSBC went and bought a lovely pewter picture frame and had it engraved with Charlie's full name and DOB – presenting it to me in order that we could put a picture of our newborn in it. It's still on the sideboard now as a constant reminder. My boss went to some lengths to find out Charlie's full name and DOB without me knowing. That was a really special moment for me and something I'll never forget.

Another TNT was when the Scottish CEO sent my wife a lovely box of chocolates at Christmas, thanking Sian for her support of me, recognising that I needed to work away from home to support the business in Scotland. Along with the chocolates was a very personal handwritten letter of thanks to Sian, penned thoughtfully and with kindness.

I used to find opportunities to call members of my team and thank them for what they were doing, asking that they take their partners for a meal and send me the bill. This wasn't usually for their performance, but to recognise something else that they had done that was of value to fellow colleagues or the wider business as a whole.

Martin Bowmer

Two Sugars?

One of my TNTs is that, in addition to remembering to make drinks for all my colleagues, I always make a point to remember how they take them.

Simple!

Alison Friel

TNT Tip Keep it simple. Simple is the best friend of consistency.

Mustang Paul

Let me tell you about a chap called Paul.

Paul is a very successful life assurance salesman – our best. He has worked hard all of his life and now enjoys the fruits of his hard work. We don't get to see him as much as we'd like as he lives at the other end of the country from where we're based.

Paul has a passion for cars – in particular, Ford Mustangs. He had just taken delivery of the Steve McQueen Bullitt special edition. Knowing this, on the day the car was delivered, I arranged for a Steve McQueen picture of him standing alongside the original Bullitt Mustang to be delivered to Paul's house from the directors of the business.

Not knowing who to thank directly, he published his response on Facebook with a huge 'thank you' saying, 'This is why I do, what I do'.

A little time, effort and thought let Paul know that, despite being far away, he is always in our minds.

Mark Ninnim

The Power of Positive Feedback

While still a junior auditor at KPMG, I had to send my completed audit file to the tax consultant, so that she could complete the company's tax computations. I included a summary sheet showing all the provisions and calculations I'd made, so that she could follow my workings and find the information she needed if I wasn't around. She called as soon as she'd opened the file to say how grateful she was, as my summary had saved her a lot of work. I hadn't given much thought to doing the summary, but it was obviously a TNT for her. As someone senior to me, she certainly didn't have to phone – I was a relative minion. She also had no formal requirement to give me feedback, but she took the time to do so. And I can still remember how good that felt, nearly 25 years later.

Once I had set up Heliotrope Learning Limited, I volunteered to be a mentor at the 'BASE competition' conducted by the Institute of Chartered Accountants in England and Wales (ICAEW). It was created to provide school and college students with a taste of what it's really like to work as an ICAEW chartered accountant, and I felt it was time to give something back. I had been allocated a team from a school in Kent – a confident, capable and enthusiastic group who insisted on calling me 'Miss' throughout the day, which was disconcerting to begin with. My role was to answer their questions as they set about the tasks in the challenge. I wasn't allowed to do the work for them but, rather, reflect ideas and suggestions back to them. At every opportunity, I tried to relate the business situation to similar scenarios in their world. I wanted to find ways to help them remember complex concepts. There wasn't a right or wrong answer, but they had to be able to justify their stance in a final presentation. At the end of the event, one of the judges who had been wandering around several tables during the task stages, noting how teams were communicating and working together, approached me. She said they weren't supposed to comment on the mentors, but she felt compelled to tell me that she thought I'd done a fantastic job with my team. She said I was 'easily the best mentor in the room' and that I had 'engaged them and kept them on track without taking over'. Well, the students seemed to get a lot out of the day, but I floated out of Chartered Accountants' Hall (ICAEW's London home) six inches off the ground. It's the power of a little bit of positive feedback, you see. Working for myself, I'm missing out on the feedback loop I had as an employee. So I really appreciated her taking a moment to tell me.

Emma Scott-Smith

TNT Thinking Be more enthusiastic about other people and what they are capable of achieving than they are themselves. Be happy for their happiness and celebrate their success. If you do this, they will want to spend time in your company, and they'll want to listen to you and to engage with you – the likelihood being that they will be far more successful. As the great Zig Ziglar once said, 'A lot of people have gone further than they thought they could because someone else thought they could'.

Passed-On Behaviours

I first heard of TNTs over 10 years ago via our company trainer Steve Sparrow when I was on a development course training to become an estate agency manager. Steve has always embraced TNTs throughout the whole time I have known him.

The first TNT encounter I had was shortly after I had transferred offices. I received a call from him on his day off to congratulate me on my prior month's performance – this really meant a lot to me at the time.

Roughly 12 years later, several years after Steve retired, he saw via social media that I'd moved on to a new company. He took the time to find out which branch and posted a personalised good luck card.

These gestures have had a huge impact on me and have greatly influenced my thinking. I now also embrace TNTs in my personal and professional lives.

Jack Downes

On the House

Having had the pleasure of meeting and working with all the wonderful JW Lees team at their annual conference, I was delighted to receive this little thirst quencher of a TNT in the post from Melanie Weatherhead!

Adrian Webster

YOU'VE EARNED A DRINK ON THE HOUSE AND AS WE'RE A BREWERY WE'D RECOMMEND A PINT OF OUR FANTASTIC CASK ALE.

However, if you're not in the mood for cask ale please enjoy any draught beer, cider, soft drink or 175ml glass of wine (that's served by the glass).

Free drink can be redeemed in any JW Lees Managed House before the end of 2018. To redeem, please hand over this voucher in exchange for your drink on us.

J.W. LEES

To Adrian,
Thank you for inspiring us to improve our Have One on Us cards to ensure a TNT moment.
Thanks again,
Mel

Keep on Knocking

I've never been out of work for any long period of time. I realise that I'm one of the lucky ones, only having needed to job search a few times in my career. I recall how stressful finding a new job was. The rejection was so tough, it ground me down. Door after door slamming in your face.

So many people post on social media that employers don't respond to speculative employment approaches. It must be so frustrating and – at times – debilitating.

Thankfully, our team members personally respond to everyone who gets in touch with us – it's the least we should do. Bad news is better than no news, I've always found.

Lately, it also made me think about our response a bit more deeply, and it stirred me to put this short message together to anyone getting in touch with us.

It has one job to do. On top of the individual response, it may reach one person on the one day when they need a few encouraging words.

I am sharing this here in case it encourages others to do the same. It took a few minutes to write, but might make a difference to one person as they search for a new opportunity.

Phil Jones MBE

Thanks for getting in contact with us.

The fact that you've put energy into wanting to join our company means a lot.

Each time someone makes that effort it comes with 'hope' of a break. That interview, new position, new beginning. We know that.

Even though we may not have an opportunity for you right now, the one thing we do owe you is a reply. This may have been your hundredth letter for all we know on a day when you feel like giving up. Don't!

Here's why.

You may not know the name Harland Sanders. In 1930, after 1009 rejections of his secret chicken coating recipe, someone finally gave him a break. 'Colonel Sanders' to give him his official title, was the man behind 'KFC' which went on to become a household name.

Keeping going when the odds feel like they are against you is what you must do. Let this short note be your encouragement.

Keep knocking on those doors, sending those CVs and keeping your activity levels up. Even though some companies don't reply, which can be really frustrating, you've done your bit.

After thirty years in business, one thing I do know is that opportunities also are closer than you think, make sure everyone you know, knows you are looking too and ask them to keep an eye out at their workplaces for you. **Lots of jobs never get advertised.** Be active in your network.

Make sure you follow our Linkedin page where vacancies tend to go first and keep up with us on social media channels so you are able to be bang up to date if called in at short notice.

I want to wish you every success in your job hunt and we'll keep your details here in case anything changes our end.

With Kind Regards

Phil Jones MBE

Managing Director

@philjones40.

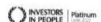

Source: Phil Jones MBE

World Class

I have been on the receiving end of many TNTs from both known and unknown champions, but this one stands out, and this is my story.

I was fortunate enough to play international rugby for Ireland during the late 1990s and early 2000s, and, although we had a modest win ratio during that time, our defeats were, on occasion, quite spectacular!

In 1998, having lost our opening match at home to Scotland 16–17 during the then Five Nations Championship, we parted ways with our previous head coach Brian Ashton, and a young 34-year-old coach named Warren Gatland was put in charge to try and instil confidence and bring back past glories.

What a baptism of fire he was walking into, as our next match up was France, away in Paris – a country we hadn't beaten away for some 26 years.

There is only so much a coach can do technically in a week, so Warren concentrated on embedding mental fortitude and team spirit as he had belief that we were good players but desperately low on morale.

The team arrived at the splendid Trianon Palace Hotel in Versailles a few days before the match. We were as appreciative of the staff and their attentiveness as we were shocked and

136

fearful – having read the French media's obituary on Irish rugby and the massacre that was about to happen that coming weekend. They were even kind enough to print the top 10 record defeats in international rugby, just so we knew exactly where we would stand on Saturday afternoon!

The morning of the match arrived, and nervous tension filled the air as we walked to our team room for our final briefing before taking the short journey to the magnificent Stade de France . . . and then it happened!

Warren stood in front of the closed double doors to the team room and said, 'Boys, no words necessary from me today, just go inside, take your time and I'll see you on the coach'.

As the doors parted and we funnelled into the large ballroom, we were amazed to see messages from wall to wall and floor to ceiling, from all around the globe, offering words of support and letting us know that no matter what, the entire country was behind us.

Messages from all ages, boys and girls, friends and family, and proud Irish people dotted in every corner of the world. We left that room teary eyed, 10 feet tall and committed to putting everything on the line to repay the faith that had been bestowed upon us and to ensure, no matter how the ball bounced in the ensuing hours, that we would earn the respect of the French and the wider rugby community.

Without giving you a full match report, and although we led at half time, we agonisingly came up short, losing the match 18–16, having emptied ourselves both physically and emotionally on the field that afternoon. But the seeds had been sown.

The foundation and platform were laid that day for future Irish rugby teams to not be suppressed by fear, no matter what the opposition or venue; to have faith in our skill, fitness and unity; and to never forget that we carry the thoughts of a nation every time we play.

Although each and every note that hung on the wall in the team room was a TNT in its own right, none would have been possible had it not been for a young, newly appointed head coach who sent an advert to the Irish press, which included our hotel fax number on it, asking for messages of goodwill and support for his boys.

A world-class TNT from a world-class coach . . . thanks Gatty!

Rob Henderson

3

Personal

The effect that a single TNT can have varies considerably from one individual to another. What could mean the world to one person may not particularly mean much to another. Out of the billions of experiences that we live through during our lifetimes, just a handful of them will remain precious to us, ones that for whatever reason remain etched in our minds. It is usually the most unlikely, fleeting encounters that end up making the biggest impacts and creating what invariably become filed away in our memories as 'magic moments'. The magnitude of the impression they make will be determined by a whole host of circumstances – where we were at that particular point in our lives, the place we were in, the people we were with, our emotions at that exact time, and how we view that specific experience within the context of everything that was going on around us when looking back.

The most powerful of all the TNTs are without doubt those that appear out of nowhere. They are the ones that are completely unexpected, random acts of kindness, whether they are from family members, friends, colleagues or strangers. Their impact can be particularly profound when they are from people with whom we have very little or no connection – these really are super-explosive, more often than not giving us a lift we didn't know we needed.

They are especially poignant because they are 100% uncon-ditional, there being no apparent benefit, obvious gain or tangible return whatsoever for those who do them. Apart from genuinely wanting to be kind, the only motivation behind taking such a heartfelt, unrequited step, for somebody that they have not met before and are unlikely to meet again, must be that it makes them feel happier. And why not!

According to neuroscientists, altruistic behaviour activates the reward centre of the brain. Endorphins, dopamine, serotonin and oxytocin are all triggered, a quartet of 'happy chemicals' that are designed specifically to make us feel great. Even the smallest of TNT acts – such as letting someone pull out in front of you in traffic, holding a door open, offering up your seat on public transport, giving money to a homeless person or putting a neigh-bour's bin out for collection knowing that they forgot to do it before leaving for work – not only elevates our own happiness, they fortify our mental well-being.

Studies have long established that, whether you are on the giving or receiving end of a gift, that gift will evoke feelings of well-being, and if like me you believe in *karma*, there surely can be no better way of creating good *karma* than by putting others ahead of ourselves. Two old adages spring to mind: 'it's better to give than to receive' and 'what goes around, comes around'.

What I absolutely do know for sure is that, when we do TNTs and we see the difference they make, something deep down inside us lights up and we experience a lovely warm glow effect. Whatever worries and anxieties we may have, are tempo-rarily replaced with pleasure and joy. The best description that I've heard for this feeling was given by a young delegate in one of my workshops who described it as being 'lit'. I'd like to stress here that I'm not encouraging people to go around doing TNTs purely for their own personal gain, nor for self-centred, selfish reasons. However, at the end of the day, as far as I'm concerned, if TNTs show empathy and compassion to the recipient and make them feel happier, whilst at the same time giving us a nice satisfying feeling, they can only make the world a better place. I think it's good to feel 'lit' now and then, even if it's us doing the lighting!

Out of the numerous studies into the effects of giving, the research that I find the most fascinating involves the ripple effect that a single random act of kindness can have. Those witnessing generous actions of others experience what is called 'moral elevation'. The comforting high that we experience from observing benevolent TNTs inspires us to behave more altruistically towards others, if not at that time, almost certainly on other occasions. In other words, it only takes one person to do one good deed to activate a knock-on, chain reaction effect, and before you know it kindness can rapidly start to spread. TNTs are contagious!

At 7 am one Wednesday morning at a Starbucks in St. Petersburg, Florida, a customer at one of the drive-through windows, having paid for her own coffee, decided to buy a coffee for the driver in the car behind. That person then returned the favour by buying a coffee for the next in line. This 'pay it forward' cycle continued on for the next 11 hours until 378 customers had bought drinks for a complete stranger!

Pay it forward is defined as the situation where someone who has had a good deed done for them, instead of repaying the kindness back directly to the benefactor, instead responds by being kind to a different person – or, simply put, when you respond to another's kindness by being kind to someone else.

Whilst on the subject of buying complete strangers cups of coffee, a TNT that seems to be becoming increasingly popular, but which has in fact been around a very long time in Italy, possibly over a hundred years – it is called a *caffè sospeso*. It is generally known in coffee shops around the rest of the world by its translation as a 'suspended coffee' or in some places a 'hanging coffee' or 'pending coffee'. It all began in the working-class cafés of Naples. Someone having experienced good fortune would order a sospeso, paying for two coffees but only receiving one.

The idea being that anyone who was down on their luck could ask later on if there was a sospeso available, and, if there was, they could enjoy a free coffee. The best way I know of doing this nowadays is for the coffee shop to have a board where customers, having paid for a suspended coffee, can leave a Post-it note with a personal message for a grateful recipient. That way, those in need of a free coffee can see if there are any to be had, and, if so, discreetly hand over their note at the counter in exchange for it.

So why, in what can be loosely termed a 'business book', am I including the following personal experiences? The answer is simple. With TNTs being so highly impactful and contagious, the ones we encounter outside of work shape our business thinking and influence our behaviours in the workplace – and vice versa. No matter what our line of work, level of seniority or juniority, we can all learn invaluable lessons and gain useful ideas on how we can improve our workplace culture. In fact, if we are true to ourselves, it should be impossible to separate our workplace and home persona – they are inextricably linked and make up who we are as a whole.

A Gooner's Thank You

Amongst the numerous letters that I used to receive at Arsenal FC, there is one in particular that stands out.

In 1984, I received a letter from the mother of an avid Arsenal fan whose favourite player was Charlie Nicholas.

In her letter, she explained that her son Russel, a 17-year-old postman, had been knocked off his moped and that, for the past seven days, had been in a coma in Homerton Hospital.

I spoke to Charlie and asked him if there was anything we could possibly do to try and help.

Charlie instantly responded with 'Let's go and visit him in hospital'.

Standing beside his bed looking at him lying there in a coma, Charlie suddenly grabbed Russel's shoulder and started shaking him and saying 'Come on Russel wake up, wake up, we're playing Spurs on Saturday!'

To my utter astonishment, and that of all the doctors and nurses, Russel's eye lashes started to flutter.

A week later, we got a call from the hospital informing us of the wonderful news that Russel was making a full recovery.

Every year, I receive a Christmas card from Russel with just two words in it – 'Thank you'.

David Dein

Uncle Pete

In March 1992, my mother passed away after a long battle with cancer. I was 19. It was tough for me being the youngest of three by six and seven years, respectively, and I found myself being on my own quite a lot.

The one thing I do remember from my mum's funeral was a large hand coming down on my shoulder and a voice saying, 'If there is anything I can do, please ask, and don't be a stranger'. The very same reassuring offer of support was extended to my brother and sister. My father, who I loved massively, was a big drinker, so his friends knew they had to help.

I carried on playing Div 2 rugby in Cardiff that season before eventually going on holiday to Newport in Pembrokeshire where a lot of the Cardiff crew used to go for the summers.

One evening, in The Golden Lion pub, I ended up getting into a bit of trouble helping out one of my close friends in a scuffle. Standing at the end of the bar was the legend Sir Gareth Edwards, and standing next to him was the man who had offered to help me at my mum's funeral.

He called me into the cwtch and started to give me the biggest rollicking of my life, 'You've let yourself down. . . You've let your mother down. . . What would she say if she was still alive?'

And the other comment which stuck in my mind was 'When you hit someone, hit them hard enough that they don't get up!'

He asked me to meet him at his home in Cardiff on the Monday, just me and him. On arriving at his house, he threw about 20 university prospectuses at me and said 'Choose a university. I am not letting you waste your life'.

Only one stood out for me, and that was the Royal Agricultural College, because it had a rugby player on the front and I also liked the idea of looking after large rural estates. I hadn't realised that, out of all of them, this was the only fee-paying one!

He told me to go and see the college (now a university) and see how I get on. My brother and I went along for the interview, and I got onto the foundation year which put me on track to do rural estate management.

Fast-forwarding 26 years, I am now an owner of one of the oldest surveying practices in the world (Farebrother – 221 years), and it was all down to the kind words and help for four years from Peter Thomas. A wonderful man who I owe a lot to.

Thank you, Uncle Pete.

Charlie Thompson

Fossils Found

Here's a TNT that blew me away. I had my 10-year-old daughter with me for the weekend, and she'd been begging to go fossil hunting with me. I'd bought her a sharp-edged archaeologist hammer, a chisel and some other tools, so we set off to a site we'd found through research online, about an hour from home. It was pretty cold, and the site was an old railway cutting that was quite exposed and used by a lot of local dog walkers. There was only one place to park by the fence to the site, and we left the car there and walked down.

After about an hour, we'd had some limited success with some small finds, but enough to really make Amelie happy with the day. Helping Amelie crack a piece of stone open, the hammer slipped and spilt my nail and fingertip open. Amelie was devastated that I was hurt, and, although I was in agony, I insisted it was okay and that we could carry on.

We walked a bit further and stopped to talk to a dog walker on the way, explaining what we were doing and how excited Amelie was at the prospect of maybe finding a small ammonite. She mentioned that she lived nearby and had seen loads in her garden when they were landscaping and was sure we'd find something. I hadn't realised my hand was bleeding quite as badly as it was, until the dog walker noticed I'd turned her wolfhound's ear red! She asked if I wanted any help with it, but I felt it would be okay, and she walked on and wished us good luck.

We got back to the car about an hour later and saw a plastic bag tied to the car door handle. I had no idea what it was, and to be honest wasn't too sure about looking in it, but I had to take it off to open the door. Inside, with no note or details, was a collection of amazing fossils, including two ammonites, one of which was the size of a saucer.

Perhaps, singularly the nicest random act of kindness I have ever experienced.

Adam Cook

Vicky

My TNT. The dictionary definition of *tiny* is 'very small, minute'. Indeed, it only took a second to swipe the inside of one's cheek to collect some minute cells – invisible yet invaluable to those needing them – place this little magic wand in the special sealed envelope provided and pop it in the nearest post box. This was the first tiny step of my memorable TNT.

It was 24th June 2017 and 30 years to the day since I had participated as a donor in a bone marrow transplant, with my adored twin sister Vicky as recipient. Vicky had been diagnosed New Year's Day 1987 with a rare bone cancer. After completing chemotherapy, she was advised that a transplant would be her best chance of survival. We were the first identical twin to twin bone marrow transplant in the UK, but tragically Vicky died in October the same year, owing to the cancer returning and this time untreatable. In the 30th anniversary year of our transplant, and coming up to our 40th birthday, a milestone I'd be sadly marking alone, I had an idea to try and get 40 people to sign up to the Bone Marrow and Stem Cell register – I put out a post on social media asking friends to sign up.

Again, the dictionary definition of *noticeable* is 'easily seen or noticed; clear or apparent'. What was initially apparent was the individual TNTs of those signing up in memory of Vicky, sending back pictures of their DIY Swab Kits and then, upon receipt of their Potential Donor ID cards, posting on social media. Not just merely 'noticeable', each one was a huge boost to the spirit, shifting focus – from all that my family had lost – to the hope that such small acts of kindness could each prevent a family from having to go through the devastating loss of their loved one. Friends started sharing the post to their friends, and I rapidly lost count of the sign-ups. The original target of 40 sign-ups was surpassed in the first 24 hours, and I stopped trying to keep track after the hundreds. It's impossible now to know exactly how many people signed up and took a minute of their time to do something great. I'll never know every single sign-up, each individual act of kindness sparked by the initial Facebook post. Many TNTs, small but powerful acts of kindness, can have a ripple effect out into the universe way beyond our knowledge of them.

www.dkms.org.uk/en
www.anthonynolan.org

Angela Henderson

Be faithful in small things because it is in them that your strength lies.

– Mother Teresa

For Féah

I ordered some clothes for Féah that didn't come.

A girl called Emily from Maidstone in Kent found my parcel that had fallen off a truck. She took a picture of my address and sent me this lovely card along with some baby grows for Féah. How amazing is she – a complete stranger.

If anyone knows an Emily from Maidstone, please tell her she's completely restored my faith in humanity.

Caoimhe Mcconway

Dear Caoimhe,

I am writing to you to let you know that a parcel you were expecting with baby clothes in will not be arriving as unfortunately the parcel must have fallen off the truck as we noticed it on the road whilst walking to school. I took a photo of your address and wanted to inform you and send a few babygros for you, which I hope fit your little one. I would have collected them off the road but they were strewn everywhere & all dirty & oily. The road is a busy one too!

Congratulations on your new arrival - always such a precious time.

Sincerely,

Emily (from maidstone, Kent in the UK)

A Load Off My Mind

I had just given birth to my daughter and was very busy trying to balance my time between the baby and my two sons, who were both under seven at the time.

Thankfully, my amazing support network of family and friends came through to help out and make this time a little easier.

As a surprise, my good friend Louise arranged for someone to collect my washing and take it away for ironing, every week for a month.

This was genuinely so helpful, and it gave me that little bit of extra time during the day to feel more like myself.

While life-changing gestures are grand, a thoughtful TNT can go a long way for someone who needs it.

Andrea Charlton

TNTs ARE THE GLUE THAT BOND THE STRONGEST RELATIONSHIPS

Happy Days

Back in the 1980s on a road trip through France, I got lost and ended up in a small town late at night. I went into a bar to see if they could direct me to a hotel. The bar owner insisted that I sit and have a drink with him and his pals, and for me not to worry about the hotel – they wouldn't even hear of me paying for a drink all night.

Many drinks later, the bar owner took me and a few of his friends to a little club owned by his sister where we played billiards and drank champagne cognac – again, my money was no good there.

Sometime in the early hours, the guy and his friends took me to a wonderful little boutique hotel and wished me a good night. I woke up the next morning and had a great breakfast; after that, I went to the reception to check out, only to be told my friends had already paid.

I can't remember his name or even the name of the town, but I hope he's having a long and happy life.

Here's another little incident that left a big impression on me.

Back in 1975, I was working backstage at the Apollo Theatre in the West End, and my job was up in the fly gallery above the stage, flying the scenery in and out. It was a blazingly hot

Saturday in August, the heat from the stage lighting was off the scale and the sweat was dripping off me as I descended the ladder after the curtain came down on the matinee.

As I reached the stage, the star of the play, Sir Alec Guinness, was standing there with his dresser, who was carrying a wooden crate. Sir Alec reached into the crate, took off the top and handed me an ice-cold bottle of Guinness.

He said, 'Here you go my boy, you look like you need cooling down'. It was such a lovely gesture I almost wept with gratitude.

Brendan Reidy

Kettle's On

Every Monday morning at 10 am, pensioner Gladys Watkins from Market Drayton, Shropshire, would have a pot of tea, along with plates piled high with buttered toast, all ready for the dustbin men's mid-morning break in her back garden. She'd have a chat with the six of them, catching up with all the local gossip and having a good laugh, which she loved. Whilst they finished off their brews and rounds of toast, she'd be out the front of the house, chucking piled up black bin bags into the back of their parked-up wagon.

When she passed away, they sent a lovely card saying how much the lads all thought of my mum. She certainly was a one-off.

Mal Watkins

Keeping It Clean

Whilst enjoying a lovely family stroll along the seafront at Hythe last weekend, I spotted this wonderful TNT.

What a great idea!

Jane Tweed

TNT Thinking Relax for great ideas. The three most likely places for any of us to have our best TNT ideas are when we are in the bathroom, out and about in the fresh air or having some fun. What all three of these have in common is that they put us is in a relaxed mode, and, as a result, in a much better place to catch some original TNT ideas. Our subconscious minds are working away 24/7, continuously bubbling up to the conscious surface brilliant ideas and ingenious solutions to problems. Most of the time, however, we are all busily rushing about, consciously having to think all the time about what we're doing or what's next on the list. Sadly, having momentarily surfaced in the conscious, the vast majority of any ideas we have silently dissipate away unnoticed, back down into the depths of our subconscious. In contrast, when we are taking a shower, going for a stroll, playing a game or having a laugh, our now-less-cluttered minds become more imaginative and far more receptive to all our creative thoughts. When we are unwinding, in addition to becoming so much more aware of great ideas, we are also in a much better position to hold on to them before they slip away – probably why so many creative people keep a notepad and pen by the side of their bed.

When you are next holding a brainstorm meeting and people start joking around and coming up with really silly ideas, just sit back and let it run. Those coming out with the most outlandish suggestions are now actively having fun rummaging around in their imaginations. It's almost guaranteed that, whenever this happens, it won't be long before someone says the magic words, 'Actually, that isn't such a daft idea!' As an old boss of mine used to say, 'The only daft idea is the one you keep to yourself!'

Hilltop Journey

My life over the last 40 years has been a procession of TNTs, resulting in innumerable serendipitous moments that have shaped new paths. Here are just a few where people have magically appeared to direct me:

I have had a curvature of the spine since the age of 12 and had practised Tai Chi for a number of years. I was fortunate that Grandmaster Chen Xiao Wang was over from China to teach in Bristol in the early 2000s. One day, he viewed my slightly twisted body in the Chi Kung 'standing like a post' pose and told me 'Buy a mirror'. This I did – and doing Chi Kung using the mirror meant that I could get in position, close my eyes and maintain the pose for five minutes or more. When I looked at myself, I discovered I had turned about 5–10° and was able to self-correct. *When the student is ready, the teacher appears.*

Having also practised Buddhist meditation, and latterly Vipassana, on and off for perhaps two decades, I was finding it not only uncomfortable but also increasingly burdensome. Eventually, I asked a friend I'd known for years who did transcendental meditation what the practise entailed. He replied to the effect, 'We just do a mechanical mantra'. This little seed became the door to my discovering this effortless method of meditation, which has profoundly affected my life for the good ever since.

I am also a big believer in the power of expressing gratitude through 'thank you' letters. When my mum died in September 2017, I wrote to the wonderful staff at Swindon Great Western Hospital and, in particular, the sweet nurse who gently touched a moist cloth against my dying mum's lips to comfort her. I wanted all the Mercury Ward staff to know that we had noticed their kindness and high quality of care for our mum, even as they performed a pressured job in a difficult situation.

I have also been fortunate enough to receive 'thank you' letters from patients who enjoyed my piano playing at Southmead Hospital, and who further appreciated the CDs I sent them of my performances. These letters came to me at a time when I doubted if my piano playing was up to much anymore, and their kindness in writing the 'thank you' letters helped me re-establish my motivation to play publicly after suffering from depression in retirement.

Vaughan Hill

Two-Wheel Therapy

In 2014, I was diagnosed with a heart condition, and I had surgery to replace a defective valve in June last year. I took the decision that it was time to leave work and start doing the things I really enjoy – so, aged 61, I did just that and retired from full-time employment.

My passion has become the great outdoors and, in particular, cycling – I have completed around 6500 km on my bike since my op. This new-found love has led me to become heavily involved in a local cycling group around where I live in Sandhurst.

I find people coming to see me in my garage at home where I provide a help service, using the skills I learnt as an engineer in the army, fixing bikes, but not just that. People come to me to talk and discuss their issues, and I discover through my own life experiences that what I plant in their heads makes them happy, and they keep coming back. My garage is almost like a surgery where people can talk openly about problems, share their thoughts and chew the cud in a safe environment.

Yes, I have my pensions, my house, my family and even a charity that I actively support – Heart Valve Voice – but my real passion is to tweak people's thoughts as well as their bikes and help them on their way. I never thought I would be seen as a wise old sage, but it gives me great joy to share my personal story and help lift the weight from some burdened shoulders with little seeds of inspiration.

Sadly, I lost my mum in May, which has made this period even harder, but I get that injection of dopamine each time I achieve a new milestone, and especially when people tell me that what I have gone through and managed to achieve has helped them.

I am delighted that my TNT story is being included in this book, even if it's just to show my grandchildren that 'gramps' is not always 'grumps'!

Ian Berry

Good Samaritan

My mum was walking the 10-minute journey to her local super-market through woodland. She tripped and fell over a tree root, hurting her wrist and breaking some teeth. Fortunately for her, a young lady who was on her way to work at the supermarket stopped to help her.

Despite making her late for work, the young lady accompanied my mum back to her home. My mum, who has dementia, called me to tell me what had happened, but unfortunately couldn't remember this kind person's name. However, she did remember that she had mentioned that this was her last day as she was changing jobs.

Armed with this information, I went to the supermarket to say 'thank you'. The staff helped me to identify her. She explained that her grandmother had had a fall a few weeks earlier, and she would have liked someone to have helped her. She made light of what she had done, saying anyone would have done the same. I asked her if she had got into trouble for being late, and she had. Sadly, she had felt unable to explain, as she thought she may not have been believed.

I offered to explain to her manager, but she declined. I gave her a bunch of flowers, we had a hug together, and I told her just how much her act of kindness meant to me and my mum. It is the TNTs that make all the difference.

Sarah Clarke

Stranger in the Night

About five years ago, my partner and I landed in Los Angeles for a holiday. By the time the shuttle bus got to our apartment from the airport, it was late at night, about 11.30 pm.

It was apparent that the shuttle had got the wrong ZIP code and left us in the wrong part of town. We were on the street in the dark with our baggage, having just stepped off a 12-hour flight, and we had been up for the best part of 30 hours.

We saw a man in his dressing gown with a glass of red wine walk by. He asked if we were okay, and as soon as we spoke, he said, 'Oh, you guys are British'.

After explaining the situation, he called an Uber for us, which at the time no one from the UK was aware of. He refused to take any money and stayed with us until the car arrived.

Just out of interest, I asked how he'd come to be walking down the street late at night in a dressing gown, holding a glass of wine. He said, 'It's simple, me and my wife just had an argument, and I'm walking around the block to cool off. Welcome to LA!'

Darren Stanton

Free Parking

Parking pay stations are not easy to navigate. I was recently in my local hospital queueing to pay for my parking after my visit. The lady in front of me was struggling with the payment, and her coins were being randomly rejected from the machine. I offered to help, and she explained that her husband was staying in the hospital for a week, and that her ticket was for seven days as it was cheaper than buying one each day.

I helped her out by entering her car details and paid contactless for her week's parking. She offered me her handful of coins, which I declined. She was extremely grateful and thanked me over and over again.

If I had managed to make her day a little better – who knows? If her husband was okay and left the hospital at the end of his stay – who knows? She was an elderly lady, and I just hope she saw it as a random act of kindness – a good old-fashioned TNT.

Paula Pattison

Merry Christmas

Whilst working as a roadie at the O2, I used to buy a homeless veteran, known locally as 'Billy the tramp', cups of tea and bacon sandwiches. I used to enjoy chatting to him.

At Christmas, Billy bought me a Xmas card.

It was a very touching moment for me, because it was someone with nothing thinking of someone else.

Adam Farmer

Kindness is the language which the deaf can hear and the blind can see.

– Mark Twain

For Me

Just short of seven years ago, I suffered a major stroke at the age of 53. It left me very weak down the left-hand side. Prior to my stroke, I was heavily left-handed.

My TNTs were relearning:

- How to put my socks on
- How to tie my shoelaces

During my eight weeks in hospital, I used crossword puzzle books and the crosswords in newspapers to teach myself to write right-handed – slowly and deliberately, using smaller puzzles to try and keep my letters within the box whilst at the same time taxing my brain for the answers. Then, when I felt I'd done all that I could, I'd fill the remaining empty boxes just to practise the lettering.

Even now I continue my recovery:

- I use cufflinks most days to force the dexterity in my left hand – I'm now working with double-cuffs
- Being a keen home mechanic/DIY person, I take every opportunity to 'fiddle' in the garage, putting nuts and bolts together – again, forcing me to use my left fingers

Andy Hunter

Feel-good TNTs

Seeing a car go by with a dog's head sticking out of the window.

Lift doors opening as soon as you push the button.

Dropping a slice of buttered toast, and it landing butter side up.

Stumbling across something you spent years looking for.

Popping bubble wrap.

Making footprints in fresh snow.

Learning something new, like why pirates wore eye patches.

Lying in a comfy sleeping bag and listening to the rain drumming on your tent.

Waking up and realising it's the weekend.

Warm sand between the toes.

The smell of freshly baked bread.

The noise of a dog's wagging tail thumping against furniture.

Clean bed sheets.

Spotting an old couple holding hands.

Watching the world pass by through the rear window of a vehicle.

The sound of an ice cream van's chimes.

Hearing a song that you once loved but had long forgotten.

The first sip of an ice-cool drink on a hot day.

Wildly guessing the correct answer to a question.

Seeing a double-rainbow.

Peeling an orange in one peel.

The evenings getting lighter.

Finding yourself at the front of a long queue.

Counting the seconds between seeing lightning and hearing the rumble of thunder.

Getting a car parking space in a 'full' car park.

A baby giggling.

The vanilla scent of an old book.

Creating shadow puppets with your hands.

Making snow angels.

Shouting 'Echo!' in an underpass and hearing it echo back.

The words 'Fancy a takeaway?'

Toll Free

Every time I was with my mate Mike and we went through the toll booths at the Dartford Crossing, he used to pay the toll charge for the person in the car behind.

Looking in the mirror and seeing their reaction was priceless, and whenever one of these complete strangers overtook us, there was always a very big smile on their face!

Martin Maytum

TNT Fact Young children smile on average 400 times a day, as compared to adults who average just 20, which coincidentally is the same number of times a person opens a fridge door on average each day!

Why Aye

My dad Stan was a born-and-bred Geordie who retired along with my mum to live in the village of Burn near Selby. He worked part time in the local pub (The Wheatsheaf) and was known well by all the regulars, until he eventually stopped about five years ago. He died in September 2019 of prostate cancer at the age of 80. The funeral was on a Friday some weeks later.

The landlord of the pub insisted on shutting the pub to normal customers during lunchtime so that friends and family could gather in the pub for the wake, despite Friday normally being their best day for trade.

On arrival at the pub after the funeral, we were greeted with a pump of Brown Cow Brewery blond ale with a picture of dad on the beer label, with the name 'Howay The Lad'.

Both things meant a lot to the family and ensured he had a fantastic send-off.

Paul Mews

Roadside Assistance

I was travelling along in my car when I saw an elderly gentleman walking slowly down the road towards me carrying a petrol can.

I stopped and asked him the obvious question, 'Have you run out of fuel?' He replied rather sorrowfully, 'Yes I have'.

I hadn't seen a fuel station for quite a few miles so I knew he would struggle to find one nearby – there were no sat-navs or mobile phones in those days.

Fortunately, due to having a temperamental fuel gauge, I had a full petrol can in the back of my old banger.

I gave him a lift back to his car and emptied my petrol into his petrol tank.

We checked if his car would start, and, after a few turns of the engine, it sparked into life. He was very grateful and offered to pay me for the fuel. I didn't take any money. Instead, I just asked him that he do the same if he saw someone in a similar situation. I can't remember what he said back to me, but I do remember him becoming emotional – I knew by the expression on his face that he would.

When I pulled away in my car and looked in the mirrors, I saw him wave and I started to well up. 'WOW', did I feel good!

Mark Shaw

No Flowers

A few years ago, on Valentine's Day, I was in my HSBC branch drawing some cash when I overheard a member of staff consoling a student who was very upset as she had no money.

The member of staff was very kind, but there was not much she could do. It was heart-breaking, so I drew an extra £50 from the cash point and, as I was leaving, gave it to her.

I had just separated from my wife at the time, and it was upsetting to see this young lady in such distress. I was struggling a bit financially myself but could always put food on the table – and besides, I was saving on the cost of a Valentine's bunch of flowers. Just wish I could have done more.

Martin

Good Neighbour

The day we moved into our current house, a warm August day some 19 years ago, we were wrestling with boxes and furniture – it was chaos, as every house move is . . . and then there's a knock at the door. It was our new neighbour, a lady in her sixties, who we had never met before. She had come to invite us to dinner with her and her husband, THAT evening – but we have two children – 'Yes', she said, 'all of you', that evening, and she wouldn't take 'no' for an answer.

When evening came, we were shattered, and so grateful for that meal. She had no idea who we were, or what she was letting herself in for – a true act of kindness.

Gill

Cheers!

I was sitting in the bar of the beautiful Roosevelt Hotel in New Orleans a year ago with my husband Jamie and our two friends, Thomas and Emily. We were enjoying late-night cocktails and chatted briefly with two guys, both Americans. It was the shortest of encounters.

They left before we did – we didn't even notice them leave, and they didn't say goodbye. When we came to settle our bar bill, the waitress told us that they had paid for our drinks!

Literally, just like that . . . made us so happy!

Was a total, no-strings-attached, random act of kindness.

BUT, it made me do my own anonymous TNT when I got back to England – made me feel so good!

Alex Meaders

Sweet Thing to Do

The winter holidays have begun, and I am preparing for my first commute home since my arrival at university. I have around 30 minutes between my last seminar ending and my train leaving to finish packing and get to the station. Last night, I handed in three essays for the end of term, and, as a result, I am carrying my own weight in hastily packed bags and running on two hours of sleep and a Diet Coke.

Problems start at Paddington when I cannot fit my comically sized bag with me through the train door and, out of panic caused by the growing, annoyed crowd behind me, I throw my bag off the train. I realise that I barely know where I am going, I don't have much time between trains and there is no way that I am going to be able to run with this impractical bag to the next platform. I have already spent an exhausting four hours on the train, yet this is just the first leg of the journey.

I have been told that London commuters are ruthless, but it is only because of the strangers who take time out of their rushed journeys home on a Friday to help me that I find my way. One older gentleman helps me carry my bag up some steep stairs and on the tube which I think is going to Victoria, I meet Tori.

I'm feeling self-assured that I have finally made it onto the homestretch, but just to be sure, I decide to check with fellow passenger Tori if the tube is heading where I think it is . . . only to find out that it is going in the opposite direction. I start to cry, and everyone looks away, apart from Tori. Even though it means going out of her way, she takes out her headphones, helps me map my journey on her phone, takes a bag handle and marches me across London via tubes and all the way to my final platform at Victoria.

She chats to me on the way, and, when she hears my stomach rumbling, she pulls out four giant bags of sweets – which she was given earlier in a product design meeting – and says that I can keep them (I am starving!). She has already shown me more than enough kindness by helping me to find my way, but this effort to lift the spirits of a stranger who feels lost and alone in London really put the cherry on the cake.

Rosie Webster

Checkout Delight

Today, when I was shopping at Lidl, a total stranger in the queue in front of me gave £30 to the checkout lady and told her to put it towards my shopping as he was trying to do one good deed a day! It paid for my entire shopping, and I was blown away by his kindness.

It was a most welcome gesture as I have had a tough couple of weeks. My husband of 45 years passed away recently, and I am having to adjust to a new life without him.

It made me realise how small acts of kindness can impact and really help someone's day. It inspired me to want to spread some kindness too.

Sue Ellway

A Personal Conception

Little short statements can change the life of millions. I am a recovered alcoholic and will be 39 years sober in October 2020.

I owe my recovery to working the 12 Steps of Alcoholics Anonymous. These work on a pivotal principle – in Step 1, 'We admitted we were powerless over alcohol. . .'; and in Step 3, we 'Made a decision to turn our life and our will over to the care of God as we understood him'. One needs to surrender and turn everything over to a power greater than ourselves – a High Power.

Now, alcoholics are rebels by nature, and believing in any 'religious' god is usually a big non-runner. Ebby Thacher, friend of AA co-founder Bill Wilson in the early days, offered a suggestion to Bill, who was then deeply concerned that using 'god' would fend-off many would-be recipients of his message of recovery. Ebby said, 'Why don't you use your own conception of god?'

This suggestion entirely transformed Bill's writings, and, to this day, 'god' in AA terms is one's own personal concept – thus, we have Christians, Muslims, Sikhs, etc., and also many non-religious members. It is the only group of people on the planet who must co-exist with complete acceptance of each another's spirituality as the result of, effectively, this one statement.

For myself, I just added an 'o', making 'god' simply the power of 'good'!

Anon

Inclusive

Four TNT examples that, for me, have made a huge impact spring to mind:

A friend of mine was suffering from PTSD, so I bought her a dozen of her favourite Glazed Krispy Kreme doughnuts – and, under each doughnut, I placed a sticky note with a message of love and positivity.

I happened to mention in conversation to another friend that my books were costing me £50 plus – and, the next thing I knew, £50 was deposited into my bank account from her.

A friend lost a baby. I donated an olive tree in the baby's name and gifted it to her. In the absence of her baby growing, this tree can grow and one day bear fruit and medicine.

In the workplace, to embrace my religion, all colleagues were invited to fast for a day during Ramadan. It was just so nice and inclusive.

Telling people of the good things you may have done should be with the right intention and not to boast, and so I share these with you in the hope that they may be of benefit to you and spark ideas for your own family, friends and fellow-workers.

M. Khan

Star Struck

We had just landed at the airport from our fantastic school trip to New York and were all slowly moving along a long corridor packed full of new arrivals having just reclaimed our luggage. I was at the back of my group of school pals when I noticed someone up ahead struggling with an overflowing luggage trolley stacked high with clothing bags and shoes boxes, some of which were toppling off and ending up on the floor. Everyone was just walking past, so I stopped and offered to lend a hand collecting and carrying a few of their belongings. I scooped up a few shoe boxes and started walking with them, and then I realised that this person was Dizzee Rascal!

I carried his shoe boxes until the end of the corridor when we reached a suitable place to stop. Dizzee was so grateful that I'd stopped to help – and, to show his appreciation, he gave me his hat straight off his head.

Owen Watkins

The Ultimate Award

When I was 11, I was playing for Cornard Dynamos Under 12s in the centre of midfield. That season, we won everything, the league and two cups. As well as being captain, I was one of the best players, and so was looking forward to our end-of-season presentation awards evening with great anticipation.

By the end of the evening, I'd won diddly squat. 'Players' Player', 'Manager's Player' and 'Supporters' Player' awards had all ended up on somebody else's shelf. I was devastated.

I woke up the next morning and went down for breakfast to find, in the middle of the table, a small wooden shield with no engravings on it. My dad entered the kitchen and said, 'That's yours boy, you did alright last season'.

Now that, coming from my dad, who was a tough East Ender who had never missed a game from when I was 6 to 16 and had only ever said 'well played' twice in those 10 years, was unbelievably emotional for me, as he knew me better than any coach I'd ever had.

My dad thought I was quite good, and that was enough for me.

Perry Groves

Our Not-So Tiny Noticeable Thing!

I had an awful time after the birth of our son. I had nine operations over a three-year period to try and fix the damage I suffered from his birth. I was continually in and out of hospital, and I was so ill. My fiancé, new baby and I lived with my parents for months, and would not have coped without them. Just as I started to get back on my feet, one of my discs shattered in my back, resulting in another few years of operations, life-long additional pain and physio – but, worst of all, we were told that I must not carry another child. We were devastated. We were desperate for a sibling for our son, so we started looking into surrogacy.

I was talking it over with my friend Roxanne during a trip to the park one day, and a couple of hours after we had left, she phoned me and said, 'I'll do it. I'll carry your baby for you'. To say we were shocked and totally overwhelmed (but grateful beyond words) is an understatement. We were aching to accept, but we wanted her to research it all thoroughly before we did. It's no small thing to carry someone else's baby!

Fast forward two years, and Roxanne is 38 weeks pregnant with our second son, and we are four days away from the C-section! It has not been an easy journey either. She has carried our boy safely through a global pandemic despite being limited physically by unexpected pregnancy-related health issues whilst working full time with two children of her own! What an absolute superhero! Her fiancé Gav has supported her (and us) all the way without a single moan.

We will never be able to put into words how grateful we are to them both. Just writing this makes me so emotional. We have battled our way through some huge lows over the past 10 years, and our extraordinary friends have given us the biggest high, the most precious gift one couple could ever give another. This baby that we have longed for – for over seven years – is our fresh start. We are so excited! We cannot wait to see him in the arms of his big brother! Friday will be a very emotional day for us all, but it is not the end of our story. Our families will continue our friendship with an increased bond and a very special addition!

Lisa and James

4

Covid

Since I started writing this book, Covid-19 has impacted every single human being on this planet. Like most, I'd never heard of it before, nor for that matter had I heard of the word 'furlough' up until recently. In such a short space of time, this terrible virus has brought unimaginable heartache to so many families and forced the global economy to its knees. Yet, despite all the pain and misery, some remarkably good things have come out of it. Social distancing may have kept us apart physically, but whole communities have been drawn closer together and entire work-forces have discovered innovative ways of staying connected and engaged. In the fight to contain Covid-19, businesses both large and small have adapted and diversified, with some even utilising their innovative skills to support key workers on the frontline. Neighbours have swung into action to care for the elderly, and children have used their boundless energy and unbridled imaginations to reach out to the most vulnerable.

There has been an avalanche of stories in the media about individuals from all backgrounds and of all ages, pulling together and doing whatever they can to help us all get through these difficult times. This awful pandemic really has brought the very best out in people. Self-sacrificing acts of kindness have come to the fore, and material objects that were once held in high esteem, now in comparison to good health, seem so superficial. The world has changed forever but, moving forwards, what lessons can be learned? The silver lining lesson for me personally is the realisation of just how important three things are – mindfulness, well-being and community – since, during 'normal' times, these sadly tend to get pushed to one side. With the world slowing and quietening down during lockdown, I have been given the opportunity to start living more in the present moment and to notice and derive pleasure from all the small stuff. Fresh air, birds singing, clear skies, plants blossoming and the occasional hum of a lawnmower are all things that, in the past, I have not paid too much attention to but am now beginning to treasure.

I've relished spending quality time with my close family, going for dog walks, sitting around the kitchen table together, and talking! Playing board games, pottering about, reading, and learning to step back and actually enjoy at times, just doing nothing. Whilst out clapping for our brave NHS carers, I found myself waving at neighbours that I never knew existed, and when venturing out, strangers across the other side of the street have been nodding and saying hello. The extraordinary key workers in the supermarkets have been all smiles, and busier-than-ever delivery drivers coming to the front door are now always up for a quick chat, albeit from a distance. TNTs have become abundant!

Even virtual meetings with clients have become refreshingly more 'human', with what were once regarded as awkward interruptions – inquisitive children, dogs barking and Amazon deliveries, now being seen as welcome distractions.

Where I live, a new outward looking mentality has emerged. Everyone has been doing whatever they can, from fetching shopping and collecting prescriptions for each other, to organising social media community groups and virtual quizzes – all pitching in and sticking together through these challenging times as best they possibly can.

What has been highlighted the most to me is just how resilient and resourceful people can be when they adapt and work together.' When we come together, when we all do our bit, and we put others first through our humble TNT actions – it is astounding the difference that can be made. It never ceases to amaze me what we the human race are capable of achieving when we really have to.

When the world does eventually speed back up again, hopefully we will look back and remember the important things that we prized so highly when all the trimmings were stripped away. My biggest hope is that we will all be a bit more flexible and open to new ways of thinking and working, and that, moving forward, we will take with us some of the kindness and camaraderie that flourished during the dark days of lockdown.

Things will never be the same as they were pre-Covid. At this point in time, whilst I'm sitting here writing this, no one really knows how everything will turn out, but one thing that I do know for certain is that, as we all continue to help each other get back on our feet and once again grow together, TNTs both in and out of work will be more relevant than ever before.

Here, in the next few pages, are just a few amongst the countless TNTs that people have been doing for each other during these difficult times.

More Than My Job

I gained a temporary position with Morrisons at the beginning of lockdown in April, primarily for routine in my life and for my own well-being, but also I wanted to help others in need in my community. I envisaged myself delivering Internet orders – but, on my induction day, that is, less than two days after my enquiry, I understood that I would be doing something different.

I quickly learnt that colleagues at Morrisons were an extended family, and I was immediately welcomed into the fold. I was to assist with the new 'Doorstep Delivery' service with Alison, a lady with a heart of gold, always thinking of others before herself. Alison and I worked very closely with each other.

As a business, Morrisons were very quick to acknowledge that many people in our community do not have Internet access or the knowledge to order online.

The vulnerable and shielded couldn't afford to wait weeks for an online delivery slot, so the supermarket set up a telephone service.

The elderly or vulnerable could phone in their order, which would be sent to local stores overnight, and the shopping was picked and delivered the following day.

Clearly, this service was well received, but I soon realised that, while the bags of shopping were important, equally vital were the doorstep conversations.

In the early days of lockdown, when people were strongly discouraged from visiting family, friends and neighbours, I was often the only visitor that some of my customers received. The five minutes' chat on the doorstep was a small window of normality for people who only got a narrow view of the wider world from the media. For those shielding, their world was restricted to their own four walls, often alone.

Following conversations with 'my' customers, I would run small errands such as posting mail, collecting prescriptions and even getting items of shopping from Morrisons' competitors with the blessing of the management. Tesco staff were amazed when I explained that I was occasionally purchasing items that we could not supply for Morrisons' customers.

I would choose greetings cards for my customers and often post them.

Having realised how much of a lifeline we were and how lonely people were, Alison and I would include little gifts in with the shopping. These might be books or puzzles printed from the Internet, or maybe chocolates or flowers, especially if we found out they were celebrating a birthday or anniversary.

It was important to Alison and me that our customers felt that they had somewhere to turn if they needed that little bit extra.

I do not know how, but Morrisons, CEO got to hear what I was doing, and personally sent me a postcard of thanks. I have to say that I was thrilled.

I couldn't imagine that such trivia reached the top level of management, and that the CEO would make time to respond.

One of Morrisons' straplines is 'it's more than our job', and many staff lived up to that.

An older couple who would definitely be described as vulnerable always came to the store for their weekly shopping every

Thursday and knew many of the staff on first-name terms. As part of their visit, they would enjoy a fish-and-chip meal and a chat with the staff. As a consequence of lockdown, the café closed, but after a little detective work by the canteen staff to find their address, they cooked and plated the couple's favourite meal, and I delivered their lunch. It was a privilege to see the joy on their faces as they took the plates and placed them on the kitchen table.

The staff were amazing in supporting local organisations and charities and would often hold events or raffles in the staff-room as well as in the store.

Personally, I didn't want to take financial advantage of the pandemic. My wife Elizabeth and I agreed that my extra earnings would be spent on those that needed help, and I think that we achieved that aim.

Bob

Inspirational Message

My daughter Samantha is a medical consultant working in the NHS. Unfortunately, she contracted the Covid-19 virus.

As a family, we were really touched to see a wonderful Facebook message from the general manager and staff at the hotel that we all stayed at earlier in the year, the Cinnamon Dhonveli in the Maldives.

Proud father

When we first heard Samantha was down with the virus, everyone was completely shocked, and they all told me that we should do something to boost her morale. Hence, the gesture was a collective one, and all were happy for the bit that they did to wish her a speedy recovery.

Sanjeeva

Superheroes

Our Divisional Commander, Chief Superintendent Raj Kohli, has offered to write a personalised letter to the children of the front-line officers here in the Met whilst they have been working through Covid-19.

It's a lovely gesture that a lot of people have taken him up on, letting kids know just how special their mum or dad are.

He got the idea from Nick Adderley, the Chief Constable of Northamptonshire.

David Hamish

Selfless

There is an amazing mum who has rallied around all the other mums at our local primary school to make up 100 'care packages' for the elderly and the isolated in the area.

Ellen Ridley collated pictures and messages of encouragement from the children, along with food, toiletries and dwarf sunflowers – she then personally delivered these wonderful TNT gifts to each and every doorstep.

What is more remarkable is that this incredible lady lost her nine-year-old daughter Jamie-Leigh a week before Christmas. Ellen is a single mum, living on her own with her seven-year-old son Alfie, who has nephrotic syndrome. She is always thinking of others.

Mums at Madginford Primary School, Kent

Chain Reaction

Last Wednesday, I woke up with that sinking feeling – it was going to be a bad day. I could just feel it in my bones. It was pouring with rain, and it was cold for the first time in weeks. I felt heavy and energyless. I opened up my messages, and my friend's father had passed away in the night. I cried for a full 20 minutes. I'd never met him, and yet I'd lived through his dying days with my friend via WhatsApp and felt part of their painful journey. We discussed how a virtual funeral might look, and I agreed to manage it for her. It would be my 14th virtual funeral in three months.

Then I opened up my calendar; overnight, two sessions for that day had been cancelled, last minute. I was almost relieved, and, at the same time, menopausal emotions rumbled through my whole body. Yep, I'd called it right. This was going to be a bad day.

Then the doorbell rang, and Mr DHL delivery man, with a big wide smile, passed me a parcel and said, 'Hope your day goes well'. That was my first TNT. He had no idea how much I needed that smile! I opened the box and – blow me down – it was a handwritten 'thank you' card and a Dutch gin bottle from one of the agencies I had been collaborating with over the past few months. It had been an intense and demanding project that we'd worked on together, with me based out here in Spain and them based in the Netherlands.

They will never know quite how special that 'thank you' was for me. It was totally out of the blue, three weeks after project completion. It could not have arrived at a better time, on a day when I most needed to feel loved, respected and appreciated. Thank you, Lepaya. You really do deserve all your success.

That buzz from opening that unexpected parcel felt so good that it shifted my mood entirely, and, with a clear afternoon ahead, I allowed myself to find some quiet. And, in that quiet, I found myself reflecting on the people I wanted to thank and reach out to. I left voice notes and sent WhatsApp messages to a handful of people who had gone above and beyond, who had had an impact on me over the past few weeks. It felt so good to make time for others in that way as I had been working at quite a pace for some time. Some sent me instant messages back, and a couple didn't reply. Then, just yesterday, one of those people called me to tell me how much my message had impacted her. We had been working closely for weeks and were so focused on work and tasks that we hadn't made enough time for the fuzzy stuff, we hadn't made the time to stop and acknowledge each other. She had had a bad day too on the day she heard my message. Like me, she felt an overwhelming appreciation for someone out of the blue thanking her for being her.

TNTs matter. They matter because they make us feel good giving and receiving them. They matter because, when we experience one, we can't help but pass on that fuzzy feeling. It's contagious. In a world full of uncertainty and unrest, we need more TNTs. Thank you, Lepaya, for kick-starting the TNT chain!

Monica Kleijn Evason

Take a Seat

We asked our staff here at Bridges Electrical Engineers Ltd to participate in a wellness survey, focusing on new routines and home-working through Covid-19.

One of my team responded positively across the board, but made reference to missing her office chair.

Knowing that she is working from home, I drove to the office yesterday, picked up her chair, drove it to her house, sterilised it, waited on the roadside and gave her a call.

The look on her face was priceless. She clearly didn't think her comments would be picked up and acted on.

Chris Maddox

An Original

My husband, originally from Port Glasgow, had always admired a Scottish artist named Alexander Millar. This year, as a surprise for his birthday, I decided to buy him a limited-edition print titled 'United We Stand'. As this was my first purchase from the artist, he advertised on his website that an additional limited-edition print would be sent free of charge. The cost would normally be £195, and the print was titled 'Heading Home'.

My purchase arrived, but with no free gift. I contacted what I thought was the gallery, but in fact by sheer coincidence I got through direct to the artist himself in his studio – charming, humorous man who had so much time for a complete stranger ringing on the wrong number! Engaged in conversation, I asked him all sorts of questions about lockdown, and he chatted away easily. I explained the situation, and he said he would arrange for the free gift to be sent – he also asked if it was for a special occasion. I gave him a bit of background and told him that my husband's childhood had been in Port Glasgow, and that some of his paintings with the men in caps and big coats reminded my husband of his male family members going to work at the port on the Clyde. I explained that it was his birthday. The artist then asked me if I would like a little personal message sent with the print – a little star-struck, I thanked him for such a generous thought and gesture.

The print and message arrived on the day of my husband's birthday. We both felt very emotional receiving this wonderful gift. I held back the tears whilst telling my husband the story. At such an unprecedented, lonely time, when all our lives are filled with sad news and all our emotions are heightened, this gesture meant so much and will continue to do so, framed in a pride of place in our home.

Debs Porter

TNTs ARE ALL THE LITTLE THINGS WE DON'T NEED TO DO, BUT *DO* DO.

Piece of Cake

My friend left a slice of cake on my doorstep today, and it's literally made my day.

If I've learnt anything from fighting breast cancer whilst at the same time trying to stay safe from Covid-19, it's to appreciate the small things in life, like a slice of homemade lemon cake!

Samantha

Workouts to Remember

Thanks to co-owner Mikey Henry, my gym CrossFit DeltaFox has been creating and dedicating workouts to members who have lost loved ones during this lockdown.

Each workout has been completed together as a gym community via Zoom, the intention being to repeat it in memory of the loved ones on their birthday.

Michael Baxter-Connolly

TNT Thinking If you want to be kind to others, start by being kind to yourself. Don't beat yourself up so much. Set aside time to step back, recharge and enjoy some 'me time'. We all have our off days, so it's worth remembering that it is okay not to be okay, and that a little self-indulgence now and then is not a selfish thing – it's actually a very good thing, not just for you but for others too. By cutting yourself some slack and caring for yourself, you'll be much better placed to look after others. As the old saying goes, 'You can't pour from an empty cup'.

Continued Support

I am a chartered town planner living in Milton Keynes, married with a three-year-old daughter. When she was born, I took maternity leave and returned on a four-days-a-week basis. I found that travelling almost an hour each way to work and the extra workload I was given made my work/life balance one I began to question. Then, out of the blue, I was made aware of an opportunity with Smith Jenkins, an independent planning consultancy in Milton Keynes, and I was invited to attend informal interviews. These went really well, and I knew this was the business I wanted to work for. I was delighted when they made me a formal job offer.

From the moment I joined them, they demonstrated their approach to supporting staff in part-time and flexible working roles which, for me, as a working mother, was extremely important.

In March 2020, arrangements were discussed about Covid-19 safe working, and when the government announced the lockdown, like many people, I began working from home. This was quite difficult, as my husband and I shared child-caring duties. It meant some long days for both of us fitting in work and looking after our daughter. Once again, I was so pleased with the support that my boss Jennifer Smith was giving me and other team members on a daily basis.

This weekend, a delivery arrived at our house. It was a hamper from Jennifer Smith and Nick Jenkins, the directors of the company, to thank me for my hard work and to tell me that they really appreciated all my efforts. As you can imagine, I was most touched by the thought and kindness shown.

It reinforced my belief that those tiny things that people do, make a huge impact.

Emily Warner

Rainbow Effect

During these uncertain times, when the world is grappling with Coronavirus, my 11-year-old daughter took it upon herself to do something to cheer up the local community.

She cut small blocks out of a piece of timber and painted them with the rainbow that is being used to signify support for the NHS.

She wrote a positive message on the surrounding edges and placed them around the village for people to spot whilst taking their daily exercise.

She hoped they may brighten up people's days.

Jo Considine

Pizza Recognition

My company sent all of us customer service advisors a gourmet chocolate pizza in the post, which was very delicious, to thank us for all our commitment and hard work in adapting to change and continuing to serve our members working from home during Covid-19.

Abby Donoghue

Locked-Down but Engaged

My company blows my mind with their kindness! My advice is: if you don't feel valued in your job, find an employer that cares about you. CDS Defence & Security consistently do the little things well, and the little things count!

They are a company with aspirations of 'Times Top 100' employer status, and really engage with their staff. Examples include a £10 Amazon voucher for all staff at Easter, a packet of sunflower seeds to add some happiness during this lockdown period, and, today, a 'thank you' card with a bar of chocolate.

If that's not enough, they have quarterly awards for staff who are nominated by other staff for innovation or contribution excellence (ICE).

There are loads more TNTs – all really great stuff that keeps me and many others engaged. TNTs go a long way!

Andy Moss

Auto Renewal

We have a car insurance policy with Admiral. Never really spent much time on car insurance, just whoever is the cheapest with a reasonable level of covid/benefits. We have been with them three years or so. Dull stuff.

But, we received an email to say that they acknowledged that there were fewer cars on the road due to Covid-19, and therefore less risk, so would be paying back £25 per car insured. We have a multi-policy, so £50.

We didn't have to do anything to get it, it was paid straight back into our account – and came with a nice, warm, fuzzy feeling. I work in the financial services world . . . so I think I'm entitled to say that car insurance is pretty bloody dull . . . but, their efforts, without needing my interaction, were wonderful. And, clever too – I'll certainly be renewing!

Chris Needham

Way to My Heart

A TNT hit me this week.

On behalf of my company, Viadex, I was having a telephone conversation with the marketing guy of a new potential vendor looking to develop a relationship with us.

We arranged to have an informal online meeting whilst enjoying a virtual cold beer together the following day. In doing so, I happened to mention a fantastic new beer that I had just come across.

The next day, a six pack of this beer (Modelo – it's amazing!) was on my doorstep along with a compliment slip. As you can imagine, I was very receptive to his pitch later on that afternoon.

Good skills, Bradley Harrad!

Elliot Read

Dry Plaice

Lovely little TNT spotted outside of Marino's fish-and-chip shop in Bearsted, Kent, today.

Just 20 minutes of rain after weeks of sunshine, and Donda the owner has provided brollies for his queueing customers during Corona.

Kirsty Patterson

Fit for Free

I was moaning to a friend of mine, Karen Turton, only last month that my local gym had closed because of lockdown. Within a few days, she had set up virtual BODYBALANCE® classes for free for her gym members and sent me an invite to join her tribe.

Four weeks later, that kind invite now has my wife, two other family members and four friends, all keeping fit with Karen, four days a week. And still all free.

My fitness has improved better than at the gym, my network has grown across the other tribe members and I remain indebted to Karen for the little things she does without thanks or payment.

Steve Nelson

Don't Know You, but
We Recognise What You Do

As a midwife during Covid-19, the shifts have a new edge. Not only are we dealing with caring for mothers and helping bring new life into the world, we are also carrying out our care with additional risk and in unprecedented conditions. Face masks and PPE may help protect, but they also keep you rather warm!

On this particular shift, on a Thursday, I left the hospital at 8 pm, just as people across the UK were paying tribute to the NHS staff by honking car horns and clapping. I drove home tired from the long day with a smile on my face, having seen and heard all the people cheering.

I arrived home 20 minutes later to see a parcel on my door-step – homemade cupcakes and a handwritten 'thank you' note from the children of a family on the new development we had moved into four months earlier. I don't know this family and they don't know me, possibly they've seen something on the community Facebook page and found out that I work in the NHS.

It was the most heart-warming, beautiful gesture. Thank you!

It's these little things that really do mean a lot.

Emily

Unforgettable

Had not seen my nan for seven weeks; she is 100 and in a care home. We were worried about her emotional well-being, so they arranged to bring her to the door so we could wave to her. Then they told us they had left a card for us on the bench outside – they had asked nan for a message and written it on her behalf.

Such a small TNT, but I cried so much. This meant the world to me; I will keep the card forever.

I work for a large academy. Last Thursday, our principal sent all staff a text at 8 pm saying he was clapping for us! He said we were amazing – a TNT that will never be forgotten!

Wendy Millsop

Whoever You Are – 'Thank You'

Last term was a particularly challenging one for all of us here at our infant school.

On top of the usual day-to-day running of the school, everyone had been working incredibly hard as a team to make special arrangements for the key workers' children, to plan staff rotas for those working throughout the holidays and to put into place special measures to make the school Covid-19 safe. They were, to say the least, difficult, unprecedented times.

On the last day of the school holidays, I received these beautiful flowers along with a lovely card containing a few very kind words. This simple gesture made it all worthwhile – not just for me but for all the team. I just wish I knew who had sent them, so that I could thank them for making us feel so appreciated.

Liz

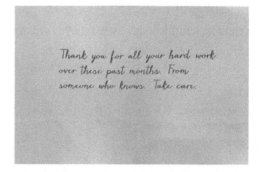

Appreciation can make a day, even change a life. Your willingness to put it into words is all that is necessary.

– Margaret Cousins

Forget Me Not

My wonderful father Keith Rosewarne died last week aged 66. For the past 10 years, he has been in charge of the Fortfield Road Allotments in Bristol, and it was a very big part of his life. Being such a sociable man with a wicked sense of humour, he had, over the years, made a lot of very good friends there – whilst busy digging, weeding, planting and chatting in his shed!

Unfortunately, due to Covid-19 restricting mourners at his funeral to a maximum of 10, none of his fellow allotment owners will be able to attend in person to pay their respects and say their goodbyes.

So, as a way of keeping Keith's memory alive at Fortfield Road, we have sent them all an 'In Loving Memory' card, along with a packet of Forget-Me-Not flower seeds inside.

RIP Dad xx

Sharon Poole

Never Too Old

I have been coaching the older generation on how to use Zoom!
Highest achiever is a lovely lady called Dorothy who, at the age of 85, is now taking part in online Pilates classes!

Sam Spillane

My Little Friend

My eight-year-old daughter Evie has a friend at school the same age as her who lives a few miles away. During lockdown, they have been talking and playing games together online. We've just had a knock at the door and found these left outside with a note for Evie.

James

Welcome Recognition

Got to say, this was a very nice gesture from the management at GAP Group Limited. Working through furlough has been extremely hard, but I was really grateful for GAP keeping me in a job.

Us five in the depot were each sent one of these today, and we were all totally shocked.

Thank you so much – especially with it being so near to Christmas, the voucher will certainly come in handy. Thanks also to Douglas Anderson, Iain Anderson and Mike Bebb.

Billy Stone

CAUTION: TNTs are highly explosive – and, like any explosive device, they need to be handled with extreme care. If you want to make the best use of them, it is imperative that you make sure of two things: that they are relevant, and that they are kept up.

If you don't, they can easily backfire – for example, if you give a bottle of champagne as a 'thank you' gift to a team member or a customer who doesn't drink. Or, having started giving everyone in your team a birthday card from the rest of the team, someone doesn't receive a card on their big day. Two well-intentioned TNTs, both having the exact opposite effect of what you were probably hoping for.

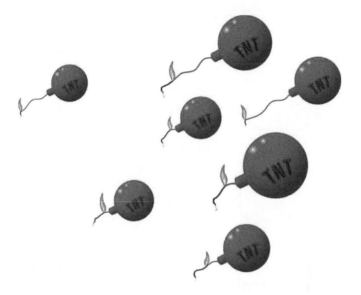

Not Alone

Having to self-isolate, my next-door neighbour couldn't have anyone visit on his birthday and celebrate with him.

So, my mum and I made some birthday cupcakes and put a candle in one, which he blew out in his front garden, whilst we, along with other neighbours, remained socially distanced, singing happy birthday and enjoying cupcakes!

Something that took very little time, but I hope made his day a bit more memorable at such a strange time.

Jo Penrose

Heroes

As the logistics manager, I am responsible for the logistics and planning around transport and traffic management on the main site here at Five Acre Wood School. In addition to all the extra new Covid-19 restriction challenges that we as a special needs school are currently facing, we have recently been met with an array of other day-to-day challenges. The school has quickly grown much larger, with a substantial increase in pupil and staff numbers. This in turn has meant a far larger volume of traffic – we currently have approximately 150 vehicles coming onsite twice a day. Myself and my fantastic team have met every single one of these challenges head on, finding solutions to logistical problems – including, at times, managing what has the potential to rapidly become a totally gridlocked site!

We all get a huge sense of achievement when we solve issues and have had fantastic positive feedback from both transport providers and parents. My TNT is from Tim Williams, the head teacher of the Loose site. One day, completely unexpectedly, he presented my team with a box of Heroes chocolates. He said that they were a token of thanks and recognition from all the senior leadership team because, in their eyes, we were heroes. This small gesture amidst all that we are going through at the moment left myself and my team 'buzzing' and feeling very much appreciated. Never before has a box of chocolates meant so much!

Sarah Eiffert

Is This You?

If you are the owner of this car and the man I saw in the petrol station this morning who paid for my petrol because I was wearing my carer's tunic on my way to work, then I'd like to say 'THANK YOU'. It was the loveliest thing to start my day early in the morning!

I didn't get your name, although I really should have. It was such a lovely gesture that has honestly made my week, and I don't want what you did to go unrecognised.

Thank you so, so much.

Hope this reaches you!

Sarah Kerr

Shop for Free

Having had an idea, on the 12th of August 2020, an inspirational local lady decided to place a post on the Bearsted and Downswood online hubs asking for contributions of food, hygiene and cleaning products to equip and set up a community 'free shop'. Lisa Marie's post was the start of hundreds of contributions by the community – the aim being to help anyone still suffering hardships during these difficult times.

On Friday, 14th August, due to a generous offer from the wonderful ladies at the Cavendish Coffee House, the dream of the shop became a reality.

A small army of 10 volunteers have collected, arranged and distributed goods every day since then. Emergency boxes are made up daily to be delivered confidentially whenever required, and the shop is open daily 9 am to 2 pm, Monday–Saturday, for anyone who needs to use it during these testing times. The volunteers are currently encouraging new shoppers to use the shop by distributing flyers and posting online.

Pam

The best way to find yourself is to lose yourself in the service of others.

– Mahatma Gandhi

Walk-the-talk TNTs

Send a handwritten letter of gratitude to a friend or colleague.
Make a music playlist for someone.
Pick up litter.
Go visit an elderly neighbour.
Volunteer for something.
Every time you buy something, give something away.

Disney Experience

We here at Magic Moments children's charity may have had to put our trip to Disneyland Paris temporarily on hold this year because of the Coronavirus pandemic, but it's still humbling to bring some cheer to the youngsters from hospices who should have been enjoying the trip of a lifetime.

So, I had an idea: if we can't take them to Disney, let's try and bring a little bit of Disney to them. I raided the Disney store online for treats and memorabilia, including embroidered cushions with the children's names.

Tiny things . . . amazing impact.

Jon Martin – chairman of Magic Moments

Cyril the Snake

In lockdown, when I couldn't concentrate on my home-schooling anymore, my mum and I used to go on a walk. Lots of people were out walking, because that was the only exercise we were allowed to do really. One day, my mum showed me a 'Community Snake' on Facebook, made of lots of colourful, hand-painted stones. I said that we should do that for our community; it was something all of my friends could easily do, and it would get them out for a walk. I thought it would bring us together when we were missing each other. So, my dad and I went out to find a big stone for the head. I painted and varnished it, and then we put it in the Woodland Trust. My mum put a post on Facebook, telling people where it was and inviting them to paint a stone to add to it on their daily walks. I called it 'Cyril'. It really took off; 212 people liked the Facebook post, and 64 people commented on what a good idea it was. Cyril has nearly 500 stones now! I was surprised that he grew so fast and that so many people wanted to add their stones. I feel proud of starting Cyril. I have taken lots of my family down to see him, and I was even interviewed about him for a local magazine!

Jude Monks, age 10

Trust

In September 2019, our youngest daughter Leya-Mae began her educational journey in reception class at school, joining her older sister Sophia, who was starting year 2. Nothing could have prepared us for the events that would follow worldwide. Leya-Mae had almost completed her second full term and was just beginning to get 'settled' when the school was closed due to the Covid-19 pandemic.

The 'new normal' was home-schooling. Both myself and my fiancée Jovita were furloughed, with Jovita returning to work in June, while I remained on furlough. We did amazing things, totally reconnected as a family and truly valued the time we had unexpectedly been given together – we were grateful. We were able to keep our children safe, able to care for them and protect them parentally – but then it was announced that schools would reopen in September 2020. There was no doubt in our minds that the children needed it, for their own mental health and well-being. One thing Covid-19 taught us is that we are not teachers, and that teachers do an amazing job. I'll never again tease my teacher friends for having 13 weeks' 'holiday' every year!

Monday, 7th September, was an emotional day. Both girls returned to school. The safety measures and procedures were clearly explained to us well in advance, all credit to the school, but the anxiety we felt as parents was heightened. For months, we'd been told by the government what we could and couldn't do, who we could meet, how many people could be there, etc., and as parents we could ensure that our beautiful girls were 'safe and protected'. All of a sudden, that duty of care was being passed to the teachers. We felt helpless. The girls were understandably anxious too.

The school were very aware that the reception class (who were now moving up to year 1) were likely to be the worst affected. They'd had more time away from school than actually in attendance. As we kissed our youngest goodbye at the gates, she was in floods of tears. Not surprisingly, she was worried, scared and without mum and dad to comfort her for the first time in six months. As parents, we could feel our eyes welling up and the raw emotion getting the better of us. We couldn't cry; we had to stay strong. We had to because we still had our eldest to drop off at a different gate, and we didn't want her to become upset unnecessarily.

The teachers then approached all parents at the gate and gave us a gift. We thought nothing of it and continued to walk our eldest to her drop-off point.

Finally, back in the car, we read the message and looked at the gifts inside. Almost with a sense of relief, we looked at each other and burst into tears. Strangely though, these were not tears of sadness; they were happy tears as a result of an amazing gesture from the school. A TNT that literally meant the world to us that morning.

Andrew

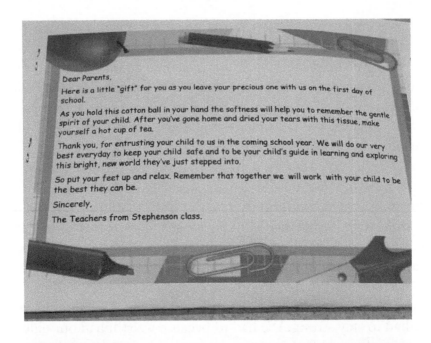

Dear Parents,

Here is a little "gift" for you as you leave your precious one with us on the first day of school.

As you hold this cotton ball in your hand the softness will help you to remember the gentle spirit of your child. After you've gone home and dried your tears with this tissue, make yourself a hot cup of tea.

Thank you, for entrusting your child to us in the coming school year. We will do our very best everyday to keep your child safe and to be your child's guide in learning and exploring this bright, new world they've just stepped into.

So put your feet up and relax. Remember that together we will work with your child to be the best they can be.

Sincerely,

The Teachers from Stephenson class.

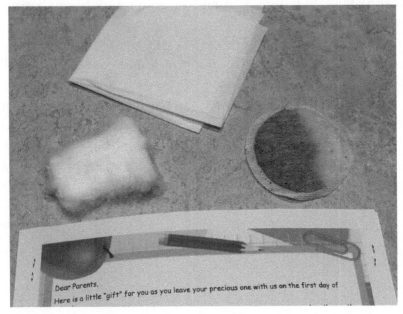

NEVER OVERLOOK THE TNTs, THEY'RE THE BIG THINGS TO SOMEONE ELSE.

Linc Cymru Housing Since Covid

TNTs are incredibly important generally in life but have never been so important as they are now. Due to our role in nursing care and the pressures we face during Covid-19 in terms of keeping carers and nurses healthy and able to attend work, we created a 70-strong volunteer group from head office to become trained and undertake day and night shifts, seven days a week.

Colleagues from our land buying team, housing, ICT, executive and myself as CEO have all worked a number of hours cleaning, washing and ironing uniforms in the laundry, supporting residents to eat meals, supporting FaceTime sessions between residents and relatives, etc. This has ranked as our greatest cultural improvement so far. The friendships created between colleagues and the respect generated through recognition of the tough job that our carers and nurses do on a daily basis is very evident. It has significantly helped to keep spirits high during these extremely stressful times.

Scott Sanders

One Last One from Me

Whilst preparing to team up with the multitalented Annabel Graham to deliver a virtual presentation to one of her clients, I happened to mention during a Zoom call how much I was looking forward to eventually getting back, post-Covid, to continuing my walk around the South West Coast Path with my old friend and walking partner, James Hill.

Having delivered my online session a few weeks later, I received in the post a fabulous book along with a very apt card containing some lovely warm words from Annabel. It is such a thoughtful gift, and I was really touched.

It has definitely made me more excited than ever about the day coming when I finally get to put my boots back on where we last left off, The Ship Inn, Porthleven!

Adrian Webster

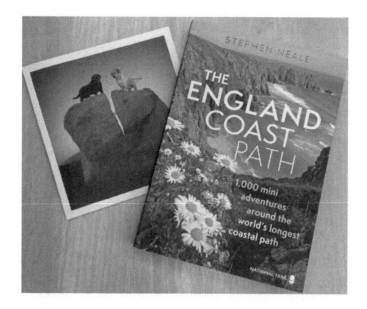

TNT Idea To help bring your team together and make a virtual meeting more fun, send out to everyone in advance hot chocolate and marshmallows. If they are not to everyone's taste, perhaps consider popcorn or doughnuts, or even ice creams, whatever takes their fancy – not forgetting to include vegan and veggie options, of course.

Special Mention for Some Very Special People

As an immensely proud patron of Five Acre Wood School, already mentioned a couple of times in this book, I wanted to extend an opportunity to all their senior leadership team to say a few 'thank yous' to some extraordinary people who once a year turn up at the school to give over 600 wonderful kids one of the best days of their lives:

> As a special needs school, we stage an annual music festival called 'Woodstock'. It's to give our pupils with profound, severe and complex learning difficulties the chance to attend a live, spectacular 'out-of-this-world' event. It is exactly the kind of festival that we all take for granted but which our pupils, given their significant needs, may never have the chance to encounter.
>
> These authentic festivals are made possible by a range of local and national organisations who kindly give us their time, commitment and resources completely free of charge. They are therefore jam-packed with explosive TNTs!
>
> Where else, for example, would:
>
> - Greggs the bakers provide 'all you can eat and drink' for everyone for an entire day

- *Morrisons, Sainsbury's, Tesco and Farm Foods donate sumptuous BBQ food.*
- *A well-known stage company (Panache Audio Systems) let us have a state-of-the-art mobile stage and technicians for the day.*
- *Professional sound companies (Gravity AV, Rory Ald Live and LTSE) source all the sound equipment and sound engineers required to produce the event.*
- *A dazzling array of brilliant renowned musicians and artists (kindly provided by several highly regarded music agencies – DeeVu, Live and Love Music, Avenoir and Tornado Productions) entertain our pupils.*
- *A local events firm (Holmsted Events) who along with the 1st Ditton Scout Group, erect huge tepees and marquees.*
- *FM Conway – provide barriers to ensure the safety of our pupils.*
- *John F Hunt Power – kindly bring along a state-of-the-art specialist power generator.*
- *Team Tutsham – offer horse riding experiences.*
- *Flair School of Dance – stage amazing dance workshops.*
- *SenSational – put on fabulous specialist themed sensory workshops.*
- *Gallagher Aggregates – who donate such wonderful things as huge boulders for people to see if they can pull out swords, King Arthur style!.*

The list goes on and on (e.g. Harley-Davidson, Kent Police, Kent Fire and Rescue and The Royal Engineers have all regularly supported us over the years).

The staggering generosity of these organisations, both in terms of their time and commitment to our school, is simply incredible; their willingness to go 'over and beyond' consistently bowls us over. In a day and age when time and money are many people's drivers, it is clear that they are all absolutely committed to giving something back to the community and providing the experience of a lifetime for our pupils. They make an incredible difference to the lives of our pupils and the entire school community, and for this we cannot begin to thank them enough.

To help you visualise the scale of these events along with some of the amazing TNTs, please search for our 'Five Acre Woodstock' film on YouTube. Please feel free to then get in touch with us if you think you can help support future events with your own TNTs!!

Thank you,

FAWS – Senior Leadership Team

Lisa and James's News Update!

We are delighted to announce that baby Mac was born weighing a whopping 9lb 11½oz! After giving us our baby and making our dreams come true, our incredible friend and surrogate Roxanne is recovering well with fiancé Gav and her own children. We will be forever grateful to them both.

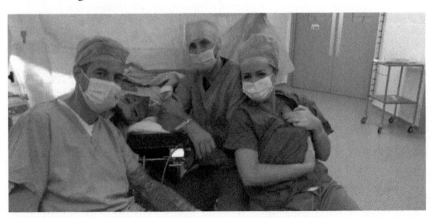

Enjoy the little things, for one day you may look back and realize they were the big things.

Robert Brault

TNTs Day – April 9th

To help promote them, I would like to take this opportunity to launch a TNTs Day!

I have chosen the 9th of April, since it was on that day in 1987 that a TNT changed the world.

Princess Diana was opening the Broderip Ward, a ward dedicated to caring for those infected with the HIV/AIDS virus at the Middlesex Hospital in London - when, in front of the world's media, and to the astonishment of millions watching, she shook hands with one of the patients there.

At the time, people were terrified of AIDS. A combination of misinformation and a lack of understanding fuelled by unbridled scaremongering stoked people's fears - it was widely believed that it could be transmitted by mere touch.

Diana's compassionate act, a handshake with no gloves, changed attitudes towards this illness.

I am hoping that every year on the 9th April you will join me along with a few others, and that we can together see what a collective TNT difference can be made in just one day, when each of us holds out a hand to someone we feel may be in need of some support.

Prize Draw: Win £500 towards a TNT experience!

To help celebrate the publication of this book, someone will receive £500 towards creating a TNT experience. All you have to do is go to my website (www.adrianwebster.com) and send me a message telling me how many times the acronym 'TNTs' appears inside this book (not including the cover).

If you answer correctly, you will be entered into a prize draw, and the lucky winner will receive £500 to put towards a personal or a business TNT of their choice.

Draw to take place on Friday, 31st December 2021.

Please note: 'TNTs' only, not 'TNT'!

Talking TNTs Podcast

Look out for my new podcast coming soon! I'll be joined by a whole host of guests as I go in search of more real-life TNTs and hopefully discover some new, innovative ways to make a difference.

TNTs 2

I really do hope you have enjoyed reading this book and that you have been as inspired as I have been by all the wonderful TNT experiences shared in it.

Above all, I would like to think that they have perhaps given you a few ideas as to how you might possibly create a few magical moments for those around you, whether they are people in your teams, your customers, your clients, your suppliers, your friends and family, or maybe even a complete, unsuspecting stranger!

However, my quest to draw as much attention as possible to TNTs and to give them the recognition that I truly believe they deserve doesn't end here. Besides my new podcast and starting up a TNTs Day, I am hoping to put together a whole new collection of real-life TNTs in the shape of another book, *TNTs 2*, in an attempt to continue spotlighting the TNTs that people have done for each other.

If you have a TNT experience that you would like to share in this new book, or know of anyone who does, I'd love to hear about it. Please do get in touch by going to the 'TNTs WANTED' page at www.adrianwebster.com.

It would be lovely to hear from you.

Thank you.

Bring on the TNTs!

There are no traffic jams along the extra mile.

– Roger Staubach

About the Author

Source: Adrian Webster

'Riot policeman', 'milkman' and 'salesman' were just a few of the entries on Adrian's CV before he moved to the IT industry and discovered an ability in himself to inspire everyday people to achieve extraordinary results.

The son of a Yorkshire coalminer, he is now an internationally best-selling business author and one of the most popular motivational speakers in Europe today – delivering keynote presentations all around the world.

For more information about Adrian's speaking or his workshops, please visit www.adrianwebster.com.